RHINO

RHINO

RYAN HARRIS

with
Stephen Gray
& Jason Phelan

hardie grant books
MELBOURNE · LONDON

Published in 2014 by Hardie Grant Books

Hardie Grant Books (Australia)
Ground Floor, Building 1
658 Church Street
Richmond, Victoria 3121
www.hardiegrant.com.au

Hardie Grant Books (UK)
5th & 6th Floor
52–54 Southwark Street
London SE1 1RU
www.hardiegrant.co.uk

A Cataloguing-in-Publication entry is available from the catalogue of
the National Library of Australia at www.nla.gov.au
Ryan Harris
ISBN 9781742708959

Cover design by Bluecork Design
Typeset in 11.5/18 pt Sabon by Kirby Jones
Printed in Australia by Griffin Press

The publishers would like to thank the following for the photographs
in the picture sections.
Picture Credits:
Private collections: picture page 1, 2, 3, 4, 6 (bottom), 9 (bottom),
11 (top), 13 (bottom) 16 (top).
South Australian Cricket Association: picture page 5, 6 (top).
Getty Images: picture page 7, 8 (top), 10, 11 (bottom), 12, 13 (top),
14, 15, 16 (bottom).
SMP Images: picture page 8 (bottom).
AAP: picture page 9 (top).

The paper this book is printed on is certified against the Forest
Stewardship Council® Standards. Griffin Press holds FSC chain
of custody certification SGS-COC-005088. FSC promotes
environmentally responsible, socially beneficial and economically
viable management of the world's forests.

FSC
www.fsc.org
MIX
Paper from
responsible sources
FSC® C009448

*I dedicate this book to Mum—miss you every day—
and to Dad, Gavin and all my extended family—my deepest
gratitude for your support. And to Cherie, thank you
for completing my life.*

CONTENTS

ACKNOWLEDGEMENTS

I would like to take this opportunity to thank the many people who have helped make this book a reality.

It has been something that I could never have achieved but for the generosity and hard work of so many individuals.

Firstly, to Dad and Gav for making themselves available to talk through the many memorable moments that we have shared in our life together. Thank you for making the time, often at short notice, to help me out, not just with this, but with everything I ask of you.

Cherie, I am grateful that you chose to be with me. Thankyou for your encouragement, positivity and counsel whenever I have come home from cricket nursing my latest ailment and feeling down on the world. There were probably a few times with this book where it felt like I was tackling some new and challenging form of rehab, but we got through it.

To Darren Lehmann, Adam Gilchrist, Greg Blewett, Mitchell Johnson and James Hopes, thank you for creating space in busy schedules and for being open and honest. I enjoy our times on and off the field.

To Kevin Sims, Damian Mednis, Peter Brukner and David Young for their professionalism, patience and care during my journey through injury and recovery, and to Alex Kountouris for his devotion to getting players back. I extend an extra big thanks to the entire medical and support staff over the years who have provided me with expert care—it's a long list, but you know who you are.

To teammates past and present—at Northern Districts, South Australia, Toombul, Queensland, Brisbane Heat, Deccan Chargers, King's XI Punjab, Lowerhouse, Surrey, Sussex, Australia's T20, ODI and Test teams—it has been a great experience made better by being part of a team. Thanks boys.

To the South Australian Cricket Association, Queensland Cricket and Cricket Australia: many thanks to the staff and directors for their whole-hearted support over the years that has allowed me the opportunity to represent my country.

Throughout these pages I have acknowledged the many coaches who have worked to make me better and to provide the guidance and wisdom that any player who aspires to reach the top must absorb and put into practice. To that end, Russell Thompson and Ian Morrison from Northern Districts deserve praise for their excellent work throughout their careers, with me and countless other young players. They are indicative of the mighty efforts of every volunteer who devotes time to make the grassroots of our game strong.

To the unflappable Pam Brewster and the team at Hardie Grant Books, thank you for having the faith in me to accomplish this book. I acknowledge your enthusiasm and support, particularly in those times when it seemed to be too big a task.

To my co-authors Jason Phelan and Stephen Gray, I greatly appreciate the many hours of hard work and late nights that you devoted to this project, and your unflagging optimism for the task. A special thanks to your families who no doubt had to make sacrifices along the way to enable the book to be worked upon when it was needed.

Well done to Lawrie Colliver for providing quick and accurate statistics when needed and to all of the professional and amateur photographers whose work is on show in these pages.

Finally, to my manager, Andrew McRitchie, who convinced me to consider doing a book, and then convinced me to actually do a book instead of just thinking about it. Cheers mate—yep, it was worth it.

FOREWORD

Who would have thought that the skinny little bloke with a cheeky grin that I used to see running around at Northern Districts in Adelaide would one day ask me to write a foreword to a book about him.

So, of course, when Ryan Harris asked me, I said yes.

Over the years I have known him, I consider myself incredibly fortunate to have been close to not just Ryan, but also his family: his mum, Gai, and father, Jim, and brother, Gavin. I know his mum would be exceptionally proud of the person he has become today, and the way he has overcome the challenges that have been flung at him along the way.

Ryan has demonstrated that when he sets himself a task to complete, he will be relentless in achieving it. As a coach you couldn't ask for more, and I am sure the fans of the game would agree. Whether it's rehabilitating from an injury, throwing himself into a seemingly hopeless cause only to force a breakthrough, or driving himself to deliver one more spell for his captain—Ryno will get it done.

It's a long way, indeed, from the bloke whose career once hung in the balance.

He has had his ups and downs, like any of us, and when it seemed as if his choices might have taken a much less successful path, he managed to change direction. He's come out the other side and has made himself a modern-day folk hero with his courage, determination and sheer force of will to overcome setbacks. He shines on the world stage doing what he does best—bowling fast and with great skill.

There's still the sense of mischief in him, though, and I hope that this side of him comes through in the book. I've had a lot of laughs with Ryan and admired him for the way he has handled the good times along with the bad.

I've been there alongside him as a player, a coach and, above all, a mate. I love him.

On behalf of Andrea and Ethan and Amy, we feel privileged to be a part of his life.

Congratulations on this tale mate, although I am certain there are a few more chapters still to come that will be worth sticking around for.

Darren Lehmann
October 2014

MY FRIEND PAIN

How many painkillers are too many? It's a question most sensible, level-headed people would probably never stop to ask themselves.

How many? A dozen in a day? Eight, ten … more?

Starting with some paracetamol when you wake up, then breakfast with a Voltaren chaser, get to the ground, warm-up … a top-up each session, then maybe some more at the end of the day when the pleasure and pain from breathtaking ice baths and boiling hot showers has worn off.

I'm aware that the humble Tupperware container I carry everywhere, with its hearty mix of prescription and over-the-counter pain relief, probably carries enough anti-inflammatory elements to put out a small blaze. Fortes? You could stage a re-creation of the opening titles of *Game of Thrones* with the fortes I can bring forth.

And you know what? The days when I don't have to take

any are definitely days I look forward to. That means all is well in the house of Harris ... or at a tolerable level anyway.

Tolerable was barely cutting it, though, when we were in South Africa for the 2014 series in March and April, which saw Australia grit its way back to the number one ranking in Test cricket for the first time in five years. After back-to-back Ashes series, one ending in disappointment, the other in triumph, taking on the Proteas at home was always going to require the team, coaching and support staff to deliver an effort above and beyond.

The hard-nosed South Africans were a lot like us: didn't like losing, had enormous pride in performing for their country and relished a scrap. Taking on the Proteas after going hammer and tongs with England to win 5–0 was a bit like an amateur boxer taking off the headgear following a tournament win ... and then climbing into a cage for some torrid MMA action with a fresh opponent.

I'd played nine Tests out of a possible ten during the 2013–14 Ashes super series—a personal milestone. As I had quipped to the media when I got back from England in August, I had achieved my goal of returning on the same plane as the rest of the team instead of being forced home early with injury.

We'd barely rehydrated and refreshed after the volley of celebrations that followed our 5–0 Ashes triumph. The celebrations had been largely unrestrained, as evidenced by a dancing Chris Rogers, for instance. 'Bucky' will never move that well again. But dusty heads had to be picked up and bleary eyes focussed on an away tour that meant more, perhaps, than even we realised.

In addition to the usual paraphernalia carried by the modern cricketer, I was also taking away a few millimetres of floating bone in my knee, which was going to be removed as soon as the series was over. My party trick was to find where it was residing in my knee, and if it was near the surface, get unsuspecting or squeamish types to press on it and see it wiggle around.

Funny huh? Well, the joke was on me the longer things went on, as it floated and got stuck or tangled with bits of cartilage and the like to 'lock' the knee. I told the media when I got back from South Africa that I couldn't wait to see my surgeon—David Young—and it was true, I'd never looked forward to an operation more.

And so, facing a long and uncertain period on the sideline once again, with my career at a crossroads once more, I got to thinking about just how I had ended up craving a surgeon's delicate and studied touch. What were those elements that brought me to where I was? I doodled some key words down as I lay in my Melbourne hospital bed and wondered what people would make of them when they picked up this book.

Numbers ... how often had that knee of mine been opened up? If I had to think about it, then it was probably too many. How many visits to a surgeon in my career?

Like just about every fast bowler, I had been diagnosed with a 'hot spot' in my back when I was around sixteen or seventeen. But the first time I broke a bone wasn't during a harum-scarum childhood, but in my twenties, on an Australian A tour of India when we were kicking a football around. It was bouncing a ball back up and missing it. Result: a chipped bone and a shortened tour.

The knee … of all things. I hurt it when I was fielding in second grade as a teenager. Nothing dramatic, just hitting the ground too hard and damaging the cartilage. A minor procedure, but one I became more familiar with the further I went in life.

Injuries. The old joke about opening the dictionary to look up injury and seeing my face there. For a while, injuries threatened to define me. We all knew about those athletes whose potential went unfulfilled due to them. Or those who fought back constantly, despite being struck down by career-crippling events. Thrice-reconstructed knees, with everything from cadaver tissue to glue to stem cells in the mix, shoulders held together like new home frames with staples, screws and wire, fused bone, scar tissue upon scar tissue.

Pain. I'm a fast bowler so it is a constant companion. But everyone has to deal with things that hurt them … and it was no different when it came to my life.

Surprises. They are great when it is your birthday, but not so good when you find a stern-looking man in blue on the other end with a serious look on his face.

Triumph. From humble beginnings, I had made my way through uncertainty and self-imposed hardships to be in an enviable position. Part of a champion team that occupied a place where Aussie fans want their cricket team to be every day of every year—on top.

So with my friend pain along for the ride, let's go on that journey. I promise to go easy on you.

CHAPTER 1

'THAT KID'S AMAZING!'

As a future chairman of NSW Cricket and a Cricket Australia board member, Bob Horsell always had an eye for cricket talent.

On this particularly sunny morning, thirty-three years ago, at a suburban cricket ground in Sydney, he was on his way to find a shady spot to sit for a spell and watch his son playing for Eastern Suburbs in a Cauwsey Shield match. But something diverted him from the action in the middle. Something small, in the shape of rather insistent toddler—as only they can be—wearing a nappy, with a dummy in his mouth, carrying a little green plastic cricket bat ... and demanding of all and sundry that balls be thrown to him so he could fiercely wield his artificial willow and whack them back.

Bob checked his stride, stopped for a bit and watched with growing amazement the prodigious mini-batsman on show. 'That kid's amazing', he offered to the lad's proud parents, Jim and Gai Harris, as he gazed in wonder at the demanding youngster tapping the plastic bat on the ground and impatiently waiting for the next ball from whichever kindly individual he had entrapped.

I always fancied myself as a batsman.

These days I would probably have ended up being recorded on someone's smart phone and shared on various social media websites with click-baiting headlines like 'Toddler plays better than (insert name of current out of form batsman here), you WON'T BELIEVE what happens NEXT!'

But back in that less scrutinised era, my single-minded display was probably due to the fact my big brother Gavin was playing, and if my boyhood hero was out there, then so was I. And when I was patiently diverted (several times) away from the playing surface and back to my own game, well, then that was the only game in town.

Gav told me that when his side were batting sometimes, long-suffering teammates would welcome a wicket in the middle so they could make an excuse (or at least risk the wrath of the incredulous toddler) to get away and pad up. Opposition teams must have fancied themselves a chance of a few quick wickets when looking over to see half a dozen blokes all kitted up ready to bat.

And a long innings would bring its own reward, spending less taxing times in the middle, while those unfortunate enough to be dismissed cheaply would suffer their own peculiar form of penance when they heard the repeated 'tap, tap, tap' and frustrated gurgling coming from over near the Harris clan.

A change of innings was also eagerly welcomed, with Gav and his mates busting themselves to get onto the field and leave me to fresh victims, usually from the opposition … I wasn't fussy. They could have been from Mars as far as I was concerned—as long as they could throw a ball at me.

I can imagine the sighs of relief would have carried across a suburb or two when my eternal innings was interrupted for a sleep in the pram.

Dad has put his hand up, though, and admitted that if it wasn't for him doing a spot of fatherly social engineering when I was a baby, then perhaps I might not have been so determined to ignore the toys I had in favour of smacking round objects with another object.

He was keen for me to enjoy sport, so when better to start than in the cradle? Apparently he would prop me up on the floor in the lounge room of our Coogee apartment, and roll a ball to me.

After a bit of this I would knock it back to him. Dad kept it up, and after a while I was grabbing the ball in my chubby little hands and shoving it back to him as best I could. By the time I was walking, I would usually have a ball nearby to kick or throw, and once I worked out how to get various grown-ups and bigger people to throw it to me, then the time would just fly (for me anyway!).

We were living in Coogee in Sydney at the time and by all accounts I was a child who enjoyed the outdoors. Sport was definitely in the genes, so it was only natural that I gravitated to playing for as long as my youthful stamina would allow. There were always plenty of kids around and Mum, Dad and my brother Gavin had a close circle of friends to ensure that the 'little bloke' always had someone to keep an eye on him.

If my paternal grandfather had not opted to seek a fresh start, I could well have been telling this story with a distinctly English emphasis. Instead of Sydney it would have been Leicester and instead of cricket it would probably have been soccer.

Our family history is like most genealogies ... a bit complicated, with gaps here and there where oral history and memory have been muddled and changed. My grandfather Arthur was from Leicester, where he and his wife Ouna lived in an up-and-down terrace house typical of the period. They raised four sons including my dad, Jim, and a daughter, and did their best to get by as many did in those days. Grandad worked with his hands as a fitter and turner and clock repairer, and the kids went to school and enjoyed the usual things kids did growing up in England in the 1950s and 1960s. Dad was the second youngest, while Alan one of his older brothers, was a promising footballer, and there was talk of a trial with Leicester City.

Dad recalls Grandad considering immigration as the children began to grow up and tougher economic times seemed likely in the future. A desire to make a better life for them was the prime motivation and the decision was made and enacted quickly. Dad says that he can remember the children being gathered and their parents addressing them on their Commonwealth of choices.

'Right, well we can go to America, Australia, New Zealand or South Africa', he put to them.

'America!' came back the universal reply.

'Right then, that's settled. Australia it is.'

So, leaving behind the rest of the extended Harris family and offshoots—I still have many relatives in the Leicester area and Dad has made a couple of visits over the years to look up great aunts and uncles and cousins and the like—they set sail for their promised land. They were among the waves of postwar immigrants known as ten-pound Poms—with adults having their fare paid for and children travelling for free as part of the assisted immigration policy run by the Australian government. More than 1.5 million people chose that option during the life of the scheme, which ran into the 1970s. As Dad tells it, the month-long voyage on the ship out to Australia was one to savour for the kids. Good weather, plenty of people to play with and ice-cream every day—the clincher for an eleven-year-old. He was among the many youngsters who were severely disappointed when the ship finally hove into port and the business of starting a new life took priority.

Like the majority of immigrants, the family lived in a hostel as they went about getting settled in their new home. In Adelaide Grandad took on whatever work he could find. An early job was as a brickie's labourer and that constituted a baptism of fire: working outdoors in the first week of January in South Australia. He was lobster red by the end of it and spent the following week in bed recovering from severe sunburn.

Grandma and Grandad opted to settle in a relatively new satellite city built on old farming land in the outer northern suburbs of Adelaide. Their choice of Elizabeth meant they could retain some of their links to their old home. It was named in honour of Queen Elizabeth II and she visited there during her 1963 royal visit.

And while they had the royal imprimatur for their suburb, the family was experiencing a more comfortable lifestyle in a newly built home, with many of their neighbours either English or Scottish and most with families. Dad said the kids loved the space they had.

Dad's never said so directly, but his enjoyment of his sea voyage at a formative age must have had some impact on him opting to join the Royal Australian Navy as a teenager. Dad joined the navy as a sixteen-year-old after a bunch of his mates at high school got talking about what they were going to do for a job. One of them said he was thinking of joining the navy. He must have been a persuasive bloke because, shortly afterwards, four of them left to enlist on the same day and Dad ended up in WA. He flunked the original exam, but remembered enough of the answers to help out one of his mates who went the next day. Another crack at the exam helped and as a career choice, it sat well with Dad. He served twenty years to the day with them, largely in administrative roles, and finished as a Chief Petty Officer.

In between any sea going duties in South-East Asia and Vietnam, Dad served in plenty of locations around the country, including Nowra. Why I mention this is that one of the funny quirks that has happened in my career is that somewhere along the way, it became a matter of 'record' that I had been born in Nowra. It still crops up occasionally in this Google-reliant world.

Now to put it on the record, my big brother Gavin was born there, but I never lived there. But we'll get to where I came along further down the track in this story.

Mum's story is a little different and one of the things I intend to do in the future is learn some more of her side of the family tree. Gai Robyn Walton was born in Kensington in Sydney where her father was involved in the racing industry (and right now there will be some people who will be having an 'aha' moment due to my, ah, *interests*, in matters relating to punting). Her dad had worked with Tommy Smith and Mum used to play with the legendary trainer's daughter, also called Gai, who is better known these days as Gai Waterhouse.

Both of Mum's parents died before I was born so I was only ever really aware of her and her older brother, John, from that side of the family. Funnily enough, Dad tells me that he used to back one of the horses her father trained, Chandos, back when he was a young bloke and was pretty surprised to see the photos from its wins on the wall of her house back when he first started going out with Mum. The world is a big place, but not as big as you think.

That's backed up for me in the way that Mum and Dad got together. Mum had introduced one of her best friends, Fay, to a young sailor named John. Now Dad had served with John on the HMAS *Yarra* and they got in touch again when both were stationed in Sydney in 1968. John and Fay were married by then and they had made plans to go out one Saturday night with Mum. Fay asked John if he knew any nice-looking single sailors on base who might be a blind date for Gai, and so John asked Dad to help him. Dad was working in the pay office at that stage and knew who was married and who was single ... but after John missed out on a few candidates due to it being short notice, he asked Dad (who was single) if he wouldn't mind coming out.

They went to the ANZAC Memorial Club in North Sydney and things flourished from there.

Mum worked for Qantas in Sydney and that's where they thought they would like to settle despite navy postings potentially interfering with those plans. They lived in Commonwealth housing in Coogee after Gavin had been born in Nowra, and spent nearly ten years there waiting for me to enter the picture.

CHAPTER 2

A SURPRISE PACKET

The surprise in Harris is that he played in four games; not surprising is the quality of his bowling. I think he's right up there with the best in the world, I really do. I think if you asked me who are the best three bowlers in the world at the minute, I'd say Jimmy Anderson, Dale Steyn and Ryan Harris. I just think he has something, he has pace, got that great length, moves the ball around and bowls a sharp bouncer. Basically it's everything as a batsman you don't want to face.

Ex-English Test captain Michael Vaughan after Ryan Harris was named as the Player of the Series for the 2013 Ashes in England.

Surprising people was something I was born to do, you might say.

Following the birth of Gavin, Mum and Dad had hoped to have more kids, but as time went by and no brother or sister came along, those dreams had dimmed to the point of extinguishment. After eight years of trying, the doctors had told them it was unlikely they would have more kids and they had accepted that their family unit would be a small one.

Then one day Mum came home with the news that she was pregnant with me. There was plenty of excitement from family and friends, and no doubt plenty of nerves for Mum and Dad with how the new arrival was going to work out. The time duly came and I was born on 11 October 1979 at St Margaret's Hospital in Sydney and went home to Coogee.

Mum was able to take time off from Qantas and when she went back to work there was no shortage of babysitters for me. Apparently I was a fairly easy going baby, and then toddler—not too much of a handful anyway. Gavin didn't mind his little brother being around either—he was old enough to have his circle of friends and activities and I mustn't have cramped his style too greatly at the time. Dad was still in the navy and was away a bit, or so I recalled, as one of my earliest memories is talking to him on the phone when he was away, probably at his last posting in Canberra.

Mum and Dad had built some close relationships in Sydney—Fay and John, of course, and Lara and Ray across the road, were lifelong friends. And so it must have been a big call for them to decide to move to Adelaide when I was four.

Dad had got out of the navy with a twenty-year pension and still had a lot of his family living in South Australia, while Mum was able to keep working with Qantas in Adelaide, so we were relatively well set to make the move. We spent a little time at my nan's place at Elizabeth before we moved into what became the family home at Meralang Avenue at nearby Salisbury Park.

Dad started work at the General Motors Holden plant at Elizabeth, which was essentially the heart of the area. As with any big industry, it seemed that everyone either knew someone who worked there, or worked there themselves. At one stage there were five members of our extended family working there. After a lot of office work with the navy, Dad was keen to get out and work with his hands in a more physical environment. He got his wish—for a fair while he would come home from the job on the line with GMH with bandaids on his fingers and hands. A lot of those seats would have had Harris DNA in them somewhere! He spent twelve and a half years there before moving on to work as a storeman for Ascot Haulage, where he stayed until retirement.

It was a stable environment to raise a family, with regular work and established schools, sporting facilities and infrastructure. Looking back now, the benefit of growing up in a community that had a lot to offer families was a major factor in shaping my approach to teamwork and going the extra yard to help out a mate.

Before too long, we were settled. Gavin was heading into high school and I was on the way to primary school, but even that prospect was something to look forward to. We had lots of cousins to play with, many around the same age, and it was in the backyards and front yards of our sports-orientated families that my exposure grew beyond my early formative attempts. For starters, I had to learn to share and, as one of the youngest, cop my share of bitter disappointments when an older, louder voice emanating from a bigger, stronger body would overrule my perfectly reasonable objections to the claimed method of dismissal.

Playing with my cousins Russell (who was just nine days younger than me), Adam, Michael and Luke was great. There was also Tim, who was between Gav and I, and Kim and Lisa, who were closer to Gav's age. It didn't matter really about the age spread: we had lots of fun playing soccer or cricket or whatever most weekends at whoever's place. Dad's brother Alan lived on an acreage and they would build go-karts that my cousin Adam and I would push each other around in and drive. They also built their own turf pitch with some makeshift nets, so as we got older we could use a harder ball. The pitch was always slow, which made it hard work as a bowler—something that probably helped shape my approach to giving it everything I had regardless of the conditions.

There would always be a big game of cricket on Christmas Day, with everybody batting, bowling and fielding. The youngest would bat and the oldest would bowl to start with and then everyone would get a go. It was fun but it was serious. A few of us played for sheep stations and I was a bit of a bat thrower when I got out, as were a few of my cousins, but we were usually pulled into line.

The fielding was always the decider—if you didn't field, then you couldn't bat or bowl. When I was a bit older and playing more organised cricket, Dad would regularly remind me to enjoy fielding. He would tell me what he used to tell Gav, which is to want the ball to come to you so you would always be part of the game. As he would say: 'You might as well enjoy fielding, because you will do a lot of it during a game.'

I learned to play initially by imitating my uncles and cousins, and Dad and Gavin and his mates. Dad was a cricket fan—he would often tell us about seeing the Windies play at the Adelaide Oval during the tied Test series—but didn't really play that much growing up. He and Mum were keen supporters of Gavin as he grew up and began to play competitively and spent most of the weekends during the season at the various grounds around Sydney. When I came along and was old enough to play, Dad would get out in the yard with us after work when he could. Gav and his mates, though, were my usual inspirations as I worked out the tricks of batting and bowling properly.

Our house was on a flat block, and the front driveway and yard was our preferred choice of venue. The drive was concrete, so I was used to playing on unforgiving surfaces from an early age. We would use tennis balls and tape them up to help them swing and to make them a bit quicker off the concrete. We didn't bust too many windows and there were plenty of local rules to make the games either fairer or harder ... I was never quite sure which. On the road on the full was out, if you hit a car parked on the road or the nature strip, you were out. If you hit a tree ... you guessed it, out! Gav convinced me early on to play straight and along the ground as that was one of the few 'safe' scoring zones. That emphasis turned out to be very beneficial later on as my game developed, although conversely it made things much tougher for me when I took up indoor cricket when I was older, as that was a tough area to score. I was usually good for a 6 off the back net at least once an innings, and plenty of caught and bowled.

It was in that cut-throat crucible of suburban cricket that I developed a deep and intense hatred of losing. Being the younger brother meant I was starting a fair way back, although I was always competitive, as was my nature. Like all kids, we liked to imitate what we saw on television, so we got Dad to help us rig up some spotlights out the back for some night cricket—white tape on the ball and some interesting shadows ... but it made for some outstanding cricket. I liked to imitate Craig McDermott and Merv Hughes when I was bowling, and Mark Waugh and Allan Border when batting. And Viv Richards ... whenever the West Indies toured he would join our imaginary front-yard recruiting pool.

I was active and into most things as I grew. We used to race our BMX bikes around a track near one of the schools and aside from a few stacks, I never realised how good I had it. From what I can compare it to, we had a really good life growing up.

CHAPTER 3

BROTHERLY LOVE

Apart from having the larger room, and being a lot better than me at pretty much all the sport we tried, the biggest influence my older brother Gavin had on me was to get a job and move away just before I turned ten years old. That set in train events that would prove to be incredibly important in my life, without me being aware of it for many years.

My early years at Salisbury Heights Primary School coincided with Gavin's time at Salisbury East High School. While I was grappling with school-work (an early confession: I wasn't always the most dedicated student), Gav was moving towards finishing his secondary education.

Primary school was a blur. I probably frustrated all of my teachers at some stage. I'd usually be talking to the kid next to me and had a poor attention span. I spent a lot of years in the front row where the teacher could keep a close eye on me. I didn't mind school but didn't like the classroom work

31

that much. I wanted to play all the time. As soon as the bell went, I would get out as fast as I could to play. I would barely eat lunch and hare off to join one of the massive games of cricket or footy or soccer that would run on the ovals and in the playground.

As you'd imagine, that sort of attitude didn't lend itself to glowing reports home. I wasn't disruptive, but I definitely wasn't engaged. If anything, I was pretty shy around people other than family. When we had parent–teacher night, I would ask Mum to go rather than Dad, because he would be the one who would be into me about doing better at school. I'd hide the report card and make sure Mum saw it first— just because she would be slightly easier on me!

I had a few good mates and was pretty friendly with most people, but I didn't enjoy being in the spotlight and being singled out, so I was happy enough blending into the pack and not catching the eye. When I did catch someone's eye, it was no surprise that it was for sport as opposed to academia.

One of the teachers, Stewart Russell, who was also the school cricket coach, found time during his patrolling of the playgrounds to watch one of the countless games of disorganised sport that would spring up like the weeds in the school oval each lunchtime. It happened that his roving eye landed on me playing against some of the bigger boys when I was in year 5, and he thought I had some promise. So I was asked to join in with the school team with the grade 6 and 7 kids. That meant interschool cricket, and so my foray onto the playing fields against other local teams also caught someone else's eye. The coach from neighbouring school Salisbury Primary, Peter Bajcic, was something of a fixture in junior cricket with Salisbury Cricket Club, our local club, and I was a logical recruit with Gavin having already been on the scene. Peter was a very important early influence on my cricket. He thoroughly taught me the basics of the game, and made sure he emphasised things like the importance of fielding, an aspect that sometimes gets overlooked in juniors with the emphasis on batting and bowling.

I was also very into soccer, with the family influence on Dad's side of things steering me in that direction. Two of my uncles, Alan and Pete, played pretty high-level local league soccer in Adelaide, and my cousins were into playing. I was skinny but fairly quick and able to get around the field without too much bother. I played all over—midfielder, defender and striker—and it was soccer that was my game in the winter rather than Australian Rules, even though I enjoyed having a kick around with the kids at school.

During the course of preparing for this book, I jotted down some of the stand-out memories from my childhood and it struck me afterwards how lucky I have been. Having both parents working, with one of them at Qantas, meant I had a relatively comfortable time of it compared to some of the kids I knocked around with. We had some great family holidays, with a trip or two to Fiji, and a memorable one to the USA when I was about nine along with John and Fay. We spent three weeks there, including a trip to Disneyland where you can't not have fun. I remember going on the boat to Alcatraz off San Francisco, and a trip to Tijuana in Mexico where it was hot, noisy and chaotic. It was a great adventure for a young fella. I also came away from Las Vegas with a favourable impression … although not for the gambling, in case you were wondering. While Dad and Uncle John were taking on the slot machines, I was at our hotel's in-house bowling alley. I bowled that much it felt like my arm and shoulder were stretched like a piece of Blu-Tack.

It wasn't long after that I had my comfortable structure shaken up with the momentous news that Gavin was leaving home. He'd been in his final year of school weighing up his options for a career or study when Mum came home with the news that there was a job going with Qantas that sounded right for him. The downside was that it was in Sydney. After agonising for a while, Gavin decided to take the job, and so within a week or so of finishing school, he was on his way to Sydney and I was suddenly an only child. Gavin stayed with Mum's brother John during that time in Sydney. John worked for St John Ambulance and stayed in the residences at the Randwick Ambulance Station near the Prince of Wales Hospital.

I missed Gav at first, no doubt. I loved my big brother but he wasn't around as much as I would have liked, especially as I got older. He would get home regularly, at least once a month for a few days, and when he was back, it was like old times, for a while anyway. We'd be out in the driveway as soon as feasible. After a while, the bangs from the balls hitting the garage roller door were getting loud enough to disturb Mum and Dad's dinner, so one weekend Dad worked out how to rig up a tennis rebounding net across the open garage ... peace and quiet reigned when one of us went fishing outside off-stump or nailed a fine leg-side glance.

Gav's absence aside, I benefitted from being the only kid in the household. I had Mum and Dad's undivided attention, and they were happy to take me all over the place on the weekends and base a lot of their social time around what I was up to.

We visited Gav in Sydney sometimes too and I would stay with him and Uncle John at the ambulance station. I hated it there. I would sleep in an old hospital bed, one of those ones that folded up, in a spare room, but I would hope we spent as little time there as possible.

Uncle John became ill when I was heading into high school and Gav helped to look after him until he died. He had never married and, unbeknownst to me, left the bulk of his estate to Gavin and I. Under the terms of the will, Gav was one of the executors and he and John's lawyer had to administer the estate until I came of age. But I was not to be informed, which in hindsight must have been bloody hard for the whole family to keep a secret from me for that seven or eight years until I turned eighteen. As I got older, I sort of knew that there was some sort of inheritance—'John's money' was a phrase I heard occasionally—but didn't really twig what it meant.

So I carried on, blissfully unaware of the windfall that was waiting down the track, and the way it would shape my attitude to money, in particular, in my future.

I was always fortunate when it came to getting things— there were the occasional hand-me-downs but by and large,

I would get new stuff. It was almost a given that when Christmas and birthdays rolled around, there would be some new sporting equipment somewhere for me. Mum and Dad were always generous—probably spoiled me a bit to be honest—and I remember that Mum used to take the approach that if you wanted something badly enough, then you should get it at the time and not worry about whether you could afford it or not. And if you couldn't get it then, then work out how you could in the future. She'd sometimes buy herself some jewellery that she couldn't afford straight out, and would lay-by it, do without something to save some money and then pay it off. I probably drew some of my own impulsiveness from that and didn't suffer too much buyer's remorse. Certainly I was more likely than Gavin or Dad to do something rash or impetuous with money, especially when I had some once I got older.

Mum and Dad were both united in their belief that when it came to Gavin and me, we should not miss out on an opportunity for financial reasons if they could help it.

As I grew and high school loomed, Mum was particularly keen for me to attend another secondary school rather than the local high school where Gav had gone. I suspect she wanted me to go where I would be challenged, academically for starters, but also where the emphasis on sport, and the resources available, would give me a leg-up.

Trinity College, a noted private school in Adelaide, had recently opened its new campus at Evanston South and that was our preferred choice. Well, it was our choice, but their choice of me wasn't so clear-cut. We duly applied on the standard application form, which had a solid emphasis on academic performance, and just as duly missed out. Perhaps we hadn't sold me on them as well as we could have.

Mum told my teacher Mr Ian Ross that we'd missed out and how disappointing it was. Mr Ross then informed the principal, Zan Majesklo, who was stunned at my fate.

'What!! But he's the best cricketer we've ever had!'

It was suggested, with some firmness, that we revisit the application and, with some assistance from coaches and teachers, highlight my level of sporting involvement at school and club level. So cricket, soccer, athletics, football … whatever could be identified. I'd had some state recognition through soccer training squads and had been playing club cricket with Salisbury, including up in an older grade. Whatever we put down must have given them a good enough reason to rethink.

I was off to Trinity College.

CHAPTER 4

'WELL, TAKE HIM AND GO!'

I've never been a real gearhead for cricket. Some of my teammates over the years (ahem, Mike Hussey) can detect the slightest imperfections in a piece of willow, seemingly identical to the one beside it, just by picking it up. Heck, with Huss I reckon he just had to *look* at it and he'd know if it was the one he'd be using to score his next Test hundred … or one that he would be quietly shuffling off onto a battling fast bowler.

I confess nowadays I do get a tiny bit excited when the tall cartons addressed to me arrive at Queensland Cricket headquarters with the latest offerings from Gray-Nicolls. It probably stems from the days when cricket was making that exciting transition from something I played with mates or at school into a more serious proposition. As I've mentioned, I didn't want for much when it came to cricket gear and probably took it a little bit for granted with what I was getting.

My junior cricket at Salisbury CC had put me into an excellent environment to grow. They worked very hard to develop their juniors and had good coaches, like Peter Bajcic, who wanted the kids in their teams to have fun and enjoy some success along the way. They encouraged the seniors and juniors to mix, which made coming through the ranks easier. It was a family-oriented club and they wanted the kids to be around the senior grades after they had finished their games. It suited the parents too, because friendships were built, and it made their trips to cricket more of a social outing and something to enjoy rather than a chore.

I played some Ray Sutton Shield matches, which was under-13s, and a bit higher than the school competitions, which challenged me. I'd had a brush with glandular fever around that time, and missing out on the various sports I was playing was always a fear because I was having so much fun, even if my competitive nature sometimes made me forget that fact.

My first fair-dinkum bat was a Gray-Nicolls Scoop. The Scoop was the Millennium Falcon of cricket bats—just the must-have bat for the era. Watching Greg Chappell use one, and then being able to get one *just like it* (or so we convinced ourselves) was like having a direct pipeline to your heroes in the Aussie dressing-rooms. We followed bat brands and trends as closely as the girls at school were following Madonna's ever-evolving fashion and music styles.

I always thought we got good bats, but it took someone who had actually used them at a higher level to provide a bit of perspective. When I was a bit older, Dad got me a Kookaburra Ridgeback from the Elizabeth Sports Store. We wanted to get it knocked in so we did what everyone did in Adelaide when they wanted cricket expertise: we headed in to Rowe & Jarman in the city.

And sure enough, Barry Jarman happened to be knocking around and so Dad and I got to talking with our host, the former South Australian Test keeper. Barry picked up the bat as we talked about getting it knocked in, put it down and promptly declared that it was far too heavy.

When Dad queried him, he was pretty adamant that we were wasting our time knocking it in for me.

'Young fella—you stand over there with your new bat', he instructed.

I did as ordered.

'Dennis Lillee is bowling, it's short! Now play a pull shot.'

Feeling slightly silly practising in the aisle of a busy sports shop in my board shorts and thongs, I did my best attempt at a pull shot off the illusory bumper from the legend of Australian fast bowling.

Barry darted over to the Aladdin's cave of cricket bats that was always a feature of the shop and came back with a different option, a Millichamp and Hall.

'Try this', he said, thrusting his choice into my hands. 'It's lighter?' I offered cautiously after few desultory pick-ups and put-downs.

Barry's eyes lit up in triumph. 'Aha!'

We went through the imagined short ball again, and I swung like before at imaginary DK, seeing him a bit better second time around. And blow me down, it felt better. A *lot* better.

I ventured this opinion to him. He nodded in a satisfied way, then went ahead and knocked in our original choice.

All was well ... until I mentioned that I'd like another bat grip put on.

'What! That's another ounce and a half you are adding on', he groused, and with his firm tone ringing in our ears that 'a lighter bat is a better bat', we quickly made our way back to the safety of the car and home.

It would no doubt please him to know that a lighter bat is indeed my preference these days, an opinion that I would happily share with any budding cricketer.

I tried to get good value for the bats I had. I knew they weren't cheap, and we did our best to get them through. We had the occasional misfire though. When I was in juniors, I was busting to use a new bat that I was sure was going to be the best ever. I was that keen to get to grips with it that the passing shower—or downpour, I can't be certain—that had swept in that day was little barrier to experiencing the awesomeness of my new piece of willow. So I used it ... a lot, happily ignoring the somewhat damp conditions. You can imagine my horror when my new stick suddenly developed a sodden lump near the toe of the bat that wasn't part of any creative bat-making process. Sorrow aside, it also meant a quick trip to the Elizabeth Sports Store to replace it before the weekend!

* * *

I was mixing up cricket and soccer throughout my high school days, but like most South Australian kids at the time,

Australian Rules football was an ever-present part of my daily life. I didn't really play AFL properly until I was about ten, but when I got into it, I loved it. I was small, skinny and reasonably quick, and could catch and kick okay. I do remember that as I got a bit older, and the opposition got bigger and the collisions got harder, I got scared of getting filled in and hurt. I kept pursuing it, though, because footy at the time was the chosen sport for many. The Central Districts Bulldogs were my team in the SANFL and we kids would happily idolise those blokes who wore the red, white and blue. One of the Centrals players, David Flintoff (who also played for Melbourne in the AFL), lived across the road from us and so he was a local legend in my books. I once met their gun full forward Rudi Mandemaker over at his place and that made my week.

When I got older, I used to love going to the Centrals rooms and having a beer after a game with them, with my mates cheerfully reminding me that I was a footy 'snuff'. I have kept my ties up with the club and have a real passion for them. I like to think I'm a loyal supporter wherever I end up—my NRL team are the South Sydney Rabbitohs and I was lucky enough to be a guest of theirs at a team dinner before a Broncos game, which was a massive buzz for me. Meeting the players, coaching staff and coach was amazing and it is fair to say that I am living up to my footy snuff reputation still. Living in Queensland, it has been tough seeing the New South Wales Blues go down to a champion Maroons side for almost all of the years I have been living here, but hopefully from 2014 onwards the Blues can create their own dynasty ... although it will be challenging.

But like for a lot of kids, options can be a blessing and curse, especially when competing interests are in place.

As I moved through high school, I was regularly playing club and rep cricket, indoor cricket and rep soccer as well as school sports like cricket, footy, soccer and athletics. Usually that worked … occasionally it didn't. I copped a detention one time when I didn't play soccer for the school on the Saturday for one reason or another but ran on for my club side the next day. Juggling was something we all got pretty good at.

I had toyed with the idea of leaving school after year 10 and maybe getting a trade (although what that meant in real terms, I had no earthly idea), but Mum and Dad were firm that I wasn't going to head down that path. What they knew, and I didn't, was that Uncle John's money was waiting for me when I came of age, and so it made sense for me to complete my schooling as my opportunities were surely going to be improved.

With the amount of time I was devoting to sport, the school suggested I do year 11 over two years: a nice way of saying I should repeat it. And it did make sense. I was getting off the bus from school and going straight to representative soccer or cricket training in town, or playing indoor cricket. I got my learner's licence at sixteen and used to drive with Dad after that, which meant I got plenty of hours under my belt in peak hour and night traffic conditions.

Up until a point, you can switch between a summer sport (cricket) and a winter sport (soccer) without too much difficulty. There tends to be the odd weekend or so of overlap, and preseason training can easily encroach into each season's turf, but as most sports are keen to keep their athletes in their camp, compromises occur and (mostly) everyone gets on with it.

Choices are never easy. I was finding that being part of a South Australian Cricket Association development squad and a South Australian youth state soccer squad was increasingly competing for the same limited time.

I was still enjoying both sports, was having some success, and really wanted to keep doing both if I could. Dad could see the writing was on the wall though, and told me I needed to make a call, and fairly soon. I wrestled and grappled with my thoughts and feelings as only a teenage boy can—black or white, A or B—and after a bit of mental sweat, made my decision. Soccer.

No, not really. It was cricket.

So Dad and I headed off to soccer training as usual one week-day evening, and after a few awkward moments, told them I was keen to focus on cricket, and that's the direction I would be heading in the future.

There was some hemming and hawing ... plenty of stern looks and the revelation that I was pencilled into the final state selection, before the frustration of losing a potential state player to a rival sport proved too much for one of them.

'Well ... well, take him—and go!' he spluttered.

So Dad took me, and we went.

It was a sad end to my soccer career, and a shame as I genuinely liked playing the game. I'm sure there are other similar tales out there, and it is a reminder that when people are passionate about their chosen game, then sometimes it can cause them to lose sight of why they play sport ... to have fun and enjoy using the skills they have learned.

Ironically, it was a muck-around game of soccer several years later at cricket training that produced one of my early serious knee injuries, but I was hardly going to sheet the blame home for that on a game that I enjoyed for many years.

Funnily enough, and without probably realising it, I had a very telling indication that cricket was my game one afternoon when Gavin came home from Sydney for a visit.

Because of shift work, and work in general, Gav had let his cricket take a bit of a back seat in Sydney. I reckon he was talented enough to have played first grade in Sydney but he was happy enough to play in the lower grades with the University of NSW, around his work.

But he was still the older brother, and as only competitive siblings can get, was happy to remind his precocious younger brother that he still had him covered. He'd got the pleasantries out of the way on arrival and we'd gravitated to the more important stuff not long after that.

We were playing some muck-around cricket on the driveway and Gav suggested he see how good I really was. We got some kit and headed off down to the local nets, the scene of many a titanic battle between big and small in the past. Gav got padded up, was ready, and with some gentle encouragement that reminded me that I was still well down the pecking order as a player, took guard.

I used to like to test myself with Gav. I was getting pretty quick by this time, certainly quicker as a seventeen-year-old than I was the year before, and so I put plenty into my first delivery. It nipped back and did him for pace, and hit him smack on the fleshy part of the inner thigh, which acts like a magnet to a cricket ball when you aren't wearing the appropriate guard (few people do when they are having a 'friendly' bat with their little brother).

I followed through to see how he was, although Gav maintains I was smirking when I asked him was he alright. He told me to piss off back to my mark and have another go.

I did and bowled virtually the same ball. He didn't get a bat on it and it cannoned into the same spot.

No smirking, I was deadset laughing by then and almost in tears when he let fly with a choice description of me and threw the bat to the ground to achieve maximum rubbing respite on the affected area.

Through gritted teeth I was invited to bat.

No warm-ups. Gav steamed in to remind me of my place. But I'd been doing a lot of training while he had been working and the odds were in my favour.

As he likes to tell it: 'After ten minutes of fetching balls from behind me and all points of the oval' we agreed to go off to play tennis instead.

I didn't beat him that time with a racket … but eventually I got the better of him, as I did with the golf clubs (although that took a bit longer). I think I've mentioned I can be a bit competitive? Gav knew how to get me to lose focus— the needle would come out and I was susceptible to a well-chosen remark on the tee, fairway or green.

Brothers, huh? Who would have thought!

CHAPTER 5

'SATURDAY, IT'S A SATURDAY!'

To borrow from The Easybeats, most of my latter teenage years were based around the adage, 'Monday I had Friday on my mind'. Songwriters Harry Vanda and George Young based their classic Aussie hit song on the weekdays they spent in migrant hostels chafing for Friday to come around when they would be allowed out. I knew what they were on about. After all, the vast majority of my high schools days were spent yearning for the weekend when sport and I would once again slot into a cosy embrace.

I'd be told time and again to do my homework before I went out for training. I used to make an attempt—but was always busting to get out as soon as I could. My good fortune was that Mum and Dad never took the lure of sport away as a punishment or disincentive. They reasoned that if I was prepared to be dedicated to sport, then perhaps the penny would drop and I could transfer some of that commitment to my school-work at Trinity College. As a theory, it was pretty sound, with the only flaw being me and my singular lack of enthusiasm about the core reason for actually going to school: to learn.

I played school cricket on Saturday and by the time I was in year 10, was playing for the first XI. I was also moving up in the grades with Salisbury and as soon as I made second grade, the school gave me an exemption to play grade ahead of the first XI.

In 1997–98, Elizabeth and Salisbury District cricket clubs amalgamated and became the Northern Districts Jets club, which played in the SACA Grade competition. A sound and sensible move for the long term, but inevitably it stirred up plenty of passions as one-time rivals became fierce allies. It didn't happen overnight but, by the time I was moving up into the grades, things had settled pretty much and there was a great sense of common purpose and camaraderie.

In any successful club, the sum of the parts is greater than the whole. And some of our sum were simply top-notch. One of Darren ('Boof') Lehmann's best mates, Craig Strudwick, was a policeman, and he was a wonderful teacher for the young blokes coming through. He was just what you wanted as a skipper. He would bat well down the order, chiming in with the occasional last-ditch rescue mission with a fresh-faced first-timer. He would bowl a few overs here and there, field in the slips, set the bowling fields, and generally orchestrate the game.

Most of the teams you played against would have had their equivalent of Struddy, so your lower-grade games would feature these wise old hard-heads facing off like chess grandmasters, wheeling and moving their enthusiastic pieces around the field each weekend through the summer. And didn't we love it! We learned by doing, and our keenness and passion were largely managed and directed.

One of the big challenges cricket has faced in the past decade has been the erosion of experience at grade level. Clubs used to be able to rely on the veterans, who often had illustrious careers in higher grades, sliding down to a level where they were comfortable. 'Ah, no love, not this season. Maybe one more year will see me out. We've got a real chance this year I reckon', they would casually mention to long-suffering partners or spouses as they searched for where last season's kit had been stashed after the prospect of them not playing was raised in the spring. Sometimes blokes would hang on for another few years because they knew their sons would be coming through into the lower grades, and the lure of playing together with their kid was a strong one for the old bulls.

As you went further up the ranks, the hard-heads were younger, but they still commanded respect. At Northern, the days when Boof Lehmann was back at the club meant school was in. There were usually plenty of rough edges to be knocked off, but once that was done, the shaping of character and cricketer would begin in earnest.

* * *

I was a fairly worldly teenager and hadn't led a sheltered life by any means, but my world was rocked in my last year of school when the club was hit by tragedy. It was early in the season, with the newly fledged Northern Jets looking to impress wherever they could. One of the other promising fast bowlers was a bloke a few years older than me, Craig Haines. He'd played in the South Australian under-19s side the previous season and was seen as one of the new wave. He'd been away playing overseas during the winter but had returned recently and I was just getting to know him.

We'd finished our regular training night the week after our first game and I recall we were discussing how he'd been tapped on the shoulder to be a net bowler for the Australians when they were next in town. The post-training catch-up was only a short one, though, as he had to head off to work the overnight shift at one of the petrol stations down on Adelaide Road at Gawler, his second night on the job.

The next morning I was at breakfast and it was all over the news that someone had been shot in an attempted armed robbery at a Gawler service station.

'Mum, I probably know them', I offered, ashen-faced, as we headed out the door, me to school and her off to work.

I didn't think of Hainsey straight away, but I was absolutely right—I did know who it was. Sometime between 2.30 am and 4.30 am he had been killed while working his shift. He had turned twenty three days earlier. The news swept around the place as we dealt with the shock, and in those days when counselling was not automatically offered at times of tragedy and great stress, it was left to the individuals and the club to rally around each other.

To make it even harder to process, it subsequently turned out that the person who was arrested, charged and later found guilty, had also played junior cricket at our club. It was a robbery gone horribly wrong. The evidence offered in court was that the bandit had got away with just $368.

When you are young and full of what is on offer, life always seems to be ahead of you. This was the first time I really grasped that life could be fleeting too. It was a huge thing for all of us. A bloke who had been sitting alongside us in our dressing-room was gone. It was like he had simply vanished between Saturdays. There was some small solace to emerge from the heartbreak, with the club and Craig's family creating a scholarship fund that would send a promising player from the club overseas to play each year, just as he had done in the months before his death.

There have been several big sportsmen's nights held over the years and I was honoured to be awarded the memorial scholarship in 2003, which helped me go to England to play. The likes of Graham Manou and another ex-Redbacks player, Chris Duvall, also received scholarships in their time and the trust continues to this day to provide opportunities for young players to grow in their cricketing knowledge. The local community still backs the event and it continues to deliver a legacy for young players who will hopefully have the opportunity, which was denied to Craig, to be as good as they can be.

* * *

The crew at Northern were a pretty tightly knit bunch who looked after their own. When I started to get some time in the top grade, the coach, Craig Bradbrook, made sure that wiser heads kept an eye on me. The skipper was Anthony Heidrich, a two-time Bradman Medal winner. He had the likes of one of our South Australian reps, Noel Fielke, a big left-hander who could whack a ball, and Boof (when he was around) to keep me and Graham Manou, former NSW and SA all-rounder Mark Higgs, and, later, Mark Cosgrove, on the right path. Dad managed the first-grade team for a while and the club stalwarts, such as Bruce Jolly, Trevor 'Buddha' Jarman and, later, Pat Cosgrove, all helped keep the place buzzing and humming.

Having chosen to concentrate on cricket instead of soccer, I promptly ended up missing some important matches due to injury. A 'hot spot' in my back meant I was not picked in the state under-17s, while an early knee injury proved challenging. All fast bowlers get some sort of injury when they are emerging—the 'hot spot' I had was either a stress fracture or reaction, or simply a spot in the bones in my back that was going to develop into something worse. The usual treatment then was rest—enforced inactivity if you will—which didn't always sit well with me. There was a bit of tinkering with my action and then an effort to get stronger through my core. As a growing boy who was still fairly slight, I was looking to improve in the medium to long term. So early injury frustrations were something I had to learn to deal with.

My knee injury had also come about in a simple fashion.

Fielding a ball in second grade, I managed to come down wrong and suddenly found myself unable to move properly. I had a minor operation (although it seemed pretty major to my impressionable self) and went about a rehabilitation that started off with the best of intentions ... I wasn't a great patient, I must admit. I tended to work on the theory that once the pain had receded to a manageable level, it was time to get back into it. Don't worry about strengthening a problem area or ensuring a full recovery time—no pain equalled time to play.

I managed to re-injure myself about nine weeks later, taking a 'speccy' up a bloke's back at school during a game of footy, and landing awkwardly. This time it required a bit more work, with more cartilage coming out. Whenever you hear a sportsman talk about requiring some 'cleaning up' of an injury in a joint like a knee or a shoulder or an ankle, it is not some clean and clinical equivalent of wiping down a bench. It tends to hurt, for starters, and you are on the sidelines for the requisite recovery period. The upside, though, is that it usually clears up the area that is causing you grief.

When you can't bowl, the one thing you always look forward to doing is getting a bat in your hands. It gives you something to look forward to. Over the course of my career, I've had plenty of chances to work on my batting. Golf was another carrot that would be dangled as a treat during rehabilitation, although my younger, carefree self would rarely have passed up a game of golf with Gav or my mates whatever stage of recovery I was at.

Fit or not, though, I always looked forward to Saturdays in summer.

CHAPTER 6

A TURNING POINT

Turning eighteen was, well, a turning point. As I grew older and the milestone of adulthood loomed larger, it became pretty apparent that instead of just a party and a few legal drinks to look forward to, I was in store for something else. As well as coming of age, I was coming into money and quite a lot apparently.

It all sounds a bit *Brewster's Millions*, I know. Mum and Dad and Gav had done their best to keep me oblivious to Uncle John's will, but things had slipped out here and there in the months leading up to my big day, and I knew that something was definitely going to change once I turned eighteen. Gav had been the executor of the will and among his duties was that I was to remain in the dark until such time as I was legal. So when the candles had been blown out on that special 11 October it was time to shed some light on what was going on.

I remember that I only took in bits and pieces the first time it was explained to me. Uncle John had never married and had no kids, so he had made the decision to leave each of us $150,000 from his superannuation. While most of my brain was 'off to the races' once I heard that figure, there was a questioning part that had something to check first.

'Hang on. Why didn't it go to Mum? She was his sister after all?' There wasn't really an easy explanation, and my question wasn't one that hadn't already been thought over long and hard. It was true that Gav and I both felt conflicted about our windfall. Gav had carried the additional burden of largely keeping a secret from me. He had used his money to help buy a property in Sydney just before his twenty-first, so it had certainly given him a big leg-up in terms of his future.

I'd gone from thinking about how I would need to get a job when I left school to save up for a car in a year or two, to being able to buy my dream car, right now, with cash.

I could just picture it in the driveway. A shiny new, top-of-the-range Suzuki Swift.

I can laugh at myself now, but at the time I thought it was the coolest thing around. Small, fast, a real pocket rocket and I could drive it to school for the last few weeks of term.

Eventually, a dash of reality arrived. Mum and Dad were both pretty adamant that while I was now a lot better off than virtually all of my mates, nothing else had changed. I still had to finish school and I needed to be ready for studying or working or whatever came after graduation. Yes, a car would be a good idea, but nothing was being rushed into.

Dad noted dryly that we needed a new pergola out the back and all of a sudden there was an opportunity to do that. Eventually I got the hint and one of the things that did come out of the inheritance was a bit of a home renovation for Mum and Dad. And it did help me think a bit more seriously about a question I had been ducking for some time. Just what was it that I wanted to do with myself once I was out of school?

Gav told me later that in my last years at school, Mum used to ring him up and after they'd got through the usual pleasantries, the topic that usually came up was what was I going to do with myself? My personal mantra 'nah nah, it's all good' wasn't much help, but Gav took the view that I would work it out, with some gentle prodding.

At one stage I thought about getting a trade and had even suggested finishing school at the end of year 10. But I made a visit to the Elizabeth TAFE to look at a mechanics course and after that, realised it may not have been for me. I wasn't sure about studying either—there was the sport side of going to university, but it seemed a bit like finishing school and then starting all over again. And I wasn't that keen. I tried it, though, and got about six weeks into a two-year marketing course before deciding again that it wasn't for me. I had been keen on maybe becoming a pilot at one stage. The Qantas influence was part of that I imagine, but maybe there was a bit of truth in the old joke about the teacher trying to motivate her students and telling them: 'Stop staring out the window during lessons because no-one is going to pay you to sit on your backside and look out a window when you grow up.' And, of course, that is where pilots come from.

So being a bit unsettled and aimless, my motivation was either going to come from within, or from an external source of inspiration. Mum and Dad saved me from any introspection by gently pointing out a few facts. The inheritance money meant that I could do anything I wanted in life. If I wanted to be a pilot, I could afford the lessons.

I reckon I responded at some point, as only a disengaged teen could, that I just wanted to play cricket because I loved it. Quick as a flash it came back at me: 'Well, love, if you want to, this will help.' So while it didn't directly go to playing cricket, it did help me in many ways. My mates were certain I was loaded, and while I was well ahead of most of them, it wasn't like I had wads of cash to flash around. I was tightly rationed for a while.

I did buy my first car. I'd picked out the one I liked and went down to the dealers to buy it. Simple stuff. Like going to the shop to buy milk. But I came back without the car. Somehow, between me walking in and waking out, the sales staff and I hadn't ended up on the same page. I was learning that being almost an adult with money was a bit more involved than first thought. I stewed a bit on it and eventually, with Mum in tow, we tried again.

I'd moved past my Suzuki infatuation and came up with the car of choice for many in the 1990s ... a Hyundai Excel. It was red (or as red as they made; Gav reckoned it was maroon when he eventually saw it). With Mum along and being prepared to pay cash, we got a few thousand dollars off the floor price, after which I was rather easily convinced to get the 'sports pack' extras. If truth be known, I ended up with all of the optional extras it was possible to get on an Excel. I then went and spent a bit more to get the obligatory sound system upgrade, including a substantial subwoofer in the back.

It did make for a tight squeeze getting my cricket kit in though. The first time Gav saw it when I went to pick him up from the airport, it took several minutes for him to compose himself.

Me (sounding a bit defensive): 'What? What are you laughing at?'

Gav (after a few deep breaths to compose himself): 'Oh nothing, nothing much. It's just that when Mum mentioned how much you'd spent on your new car, I was expecting you to arrive in a big Holden V8 ... not a hairdresser's car.'

I scornfully told him that he was missing the point and that, in fact, it was a very 'now' car to have. So anyway, when we tried to squeeze his bags in, he lost it again.

I know he was only trying to wind me up, and I hardly bit at all. Anyway, it was fun to drive and my mates and I enjoyed cruising around town in it. Well, me and whoever else could fit in.

* * *

I finished school with a reasonable score, although nothing that cried out for me to try academia. I moved into the work force and basically found myself doing a number of part-time jobs, none for terribly long, and usually revolving around cricket. I delivered gas for a while, worked in a sports store in

Salisbury, helped out with cleaning street sweepers (a job as dirty as it sounds). I tended to stick at the jobs but knew that when it came down to it, I would pursue whatever cricket opportunities I could. Having money in the bank allayed the usual fears and concerns a person in my position might have had. I still had to make it as a cricketer … but the security net was there that others in my position might not have had.

Despite everyone's best intentions, though, I did spend a fair bit of the windfall in my early years. At one stage I told Dad that I thought I had wasted the money, but he thought otherwise. I was growing up and while I had some advantages that others didn't I was like everyone else learning how to manage money. As he pointed out, thanks to Uncle John's generosity, I had a car and, later, my first house (which I still own at Ingle Farm). I turned out the person I would be regardless of the money, but it did free me up to indulge my love of cricket and chase my dream of making it my career.

Skip forward a few seasons and my first contract with the SACA as a twenty-year-old was for $12,500—cricket was always going to be a slow burn financially. In fact, being a state-level cricketer really wasn't financially viable unless you played for a lot of seasons at or near the top bracket in the state system, or cracked it to play for Australia and earn (and more importantly keep) a central contract. The Australian Cricketers' Association's negotiations with Cricket Australia during the 1990s had delivered more financial security than ever before for cricketers, but it wasn't easy street. Part-time or full-time work was still very much on the cards for those players either on the fringe or making their way up the ladder.

The 'learn or earn' policy was in vogue around the states, encouraging players not to rely just on their cricket skills and, to an extent, it was sound advice. Not that everyone followed it, but for those who did, it reminded them that any sporting career was fleeting at best and there were an awful lot of years after your playing days ended that needed to be addressed.

Looking back now, I know I was bloody lucky. Not only did I get a leg-up at a stage of my life where I was just supposed to be starting out, I was also able to focus on doing something that required a lot of outlay in terms of time and commitment, and still have some security to fall back on. So a turning point indeed, even if my change of direction then proceeded to twist and turn in ways my teenage self could not have imagined.

CHAPTER 7

TWENTY-ONE TODAY

'Happy birthday Chicksy, you're going to make your debut for the Redbacks. Now, it's not official yet, so keep it quiet okay. Don't tell too many people. Going to be a fun night, hey.'

Yeah, yeah, yeah, yeah—WHAT?

Wow, where was I supposed to start? Oh wait, that's right, it was my *twenty-first birthday party* and I was being asked to be a bit discreet with some massive news.

I was certainly very grateful when Boof and Greg Blewett took me aside behind the gazebo and let me into their confidence early in October 2000, and agreed immediately that I would keep it to myself. Okay, sure, tell Mum and Dad, and Gav, and maybe Uncle John and Aunty Fay and the boys from Northern …

As you can see from the photo of that night elsewhere in this book, I was a happy fella. I'm sure my speech was a doozy. From what I recall, it seemed to go off okay.

We'd organised my twenty-first for the first weekend in October, which turned out to be excellent timing with my debut set down for the next weekend, three days before my actual birthday.

I was to wear the Redbacks colours for the first time against Queensland in Brisbane. It was at Allan Border Field rather than the Gabba, which was unavailable due to the Sydney Olympics. It didn't bother me, especially when I got there and found it more like the club grounds that I was used to as opposed to a big stadium like the Gabba.

I was a bit nervous, especially going up against a Bulls side that had the likes of Matthew Hayden, Jimmy Maher, Martin Love, Stuart Law and Andy Bichel in it. But alongside Blewey, Boof, Graham Manou and Paul 'Blocker' Wilson, I had every reason to be confident.

It was a beaut day, with a good-sized crowd that felt like they were almost on the field with you at times. I didn't have much time to settle as we won the toss and sent the Bulls in to bat, hoping to get some early life out of what was a typically sound one-day track at their home away from home. After a few overs from Mark Harrity and Blocker, the ball was tossed to me and away I went ... bowling to the intimidating Matthew Hayden. But I got some nice shape with the newish ball and away went Haydos, caught behind and grousing all the way to the rooms ('Why didn't *someone* say he bowled an outswinger?'). It worked for one big gun, so I tried much the same to Stu Law, with the same result as he went to drive.

Two in two! How good is that at interstate cricket? A hat-trick? Could I dare to dream? And then Martin Love languidly moved to the wicket, casually took strike, and effortlessly handled the hat-trick ball. And quite a few more after that. He and Jimmy Maher scored 60s and with some Bichel big hitting and other contributions down the order, Queensland finished with 7–273. It was a handy score, but one that might have been 30 runs short on the compact Border Field, with its short square boundaries. I had 2–35 from 7 overs, so was well pleased that Boof had looked after me, and that I had done my job to get wickets at the top of the order.

As a debut, I couldn't really complain. We were in a bit of strife at 6–195 when 'Choc' Manou got out and I ended up in a partnership with Ben Johnson that took us to within striking distance of chasing down the runs. I'd hit someone for a few funs and Haydos decided enough was enough and hopped into me from point. Someone, maybe Boof, could have suggested to me that if any of the old hard-heads from Queensland went at me, then the best thing to do was to be quiet. I'm not sure I quite got that right. The scene was set an over or so later when Haydos came in to bowl, robust medium-pacers I recall. He dropped one short and I went hard to pull it, only to misjudge the pace and sky it straight up in the air and be caught. That was it for the day for me, and after a thrilling last few overs, we fell 3 runs short.

The Queenslanders were tough, but they also demonstrated similar qualities to the ones that Boof had always espoused and now the Redbacks had already displayed for me. Play hard on the field, and then have a beer and a friendly yarn afterwards. It was a telling reminder to me that while it was a step up from grade cricket, there were plenty of similarities in how we played the game. Most of the states got on with Queensland, just as they did with South Australia and Western Australia. The Vics and NSW would be a bit harder to crack, as was Tassie for a while, and as I gained experience, I knew the games that each state would be 'up' for. I remember Mike Hussey saying something similar many years later about how he had hated playing Queensland. There would always be a Matt Hayden or an Andrew Symonds or Stuart Law or someone who would be into him when he came to bat for WA and, more often than not, he would miss out and their words would ring in his ears all the way back to the rooms. And then at the end of the game, they would be great company and as it turned out, good teammates when several of them ended up in the Australia team set-up.

I was fortunate to be able to follow my one-day debut with an encore performance the following week against Tasmania. I was twenty-one for real this time, and again, found myself in a match that had plenty to teach me. Overnight rain in Adelaide meant a delayed start, so the game was reduced to 43 overs a side, with the threat of more bad weather around. The Tigers sent us in and we performed solidly to score 6–248. No batting for me this time so when I got the ball, I was naturally anxious to recapture my debut effort and show I was worth having around. Unfortunately I (and most of the attack) ended up copping some stick from two of Tassie's finest: the heavy-scoring left-hander Michael Di Venuto (124) and young Ricky Ponting (68). I was involved in the run-out that removed Diva, and with the team holding its collective nerve, we won by 4 runs. Being part of an exciting win in front of friends and family was more than enough to convince me that I had made the right choice; the question now was how much more of this could I have.

I went on to play five more games that season, and found that the learning curve as a rookie state cricketer was steeper than anything I had ever encountered. I had another rain-affected game against the Victorians that we won well, and then pinched a thriller over NSW at the North Sydney Oval. That was a game where I had the best seat in the house as the non-striker looking on from the other end of the pitch as Boof scored one of his typically inventive centuries. My 31 not out was not even on the radar compared to his 115 off 118 balls, but I thoroughly enjoyed being the first person to celebrate his ton when he brought up three figures against a steady NSW attack consisting of Glenn McGrath, Brett Lee, Nathan Bracken, Stuart MacGill ...

No wonder I was enjoying the moment. Looking on at the larrikin kid enjoying the reflected glory of Boof's hundred were the likes of Steve Waugh, Mark Waugh, Michael Slater, Michael Bevan and a handy young keeper by the name of Brad Haddin. No-one else quite did star-studded like NSW in those days on the rare occasions when they had their Aussie players to call upon. Despite the stellar cast, the Redbacks triumphed on that occasion.

Any young player coming through the ranks early in their career is going to have a moment like that. Suddenly the blokes you had been cheering for on the television were right there in front of you, usually doing everything in their power to remind you of your place and role in this game. That is, down the bottom, and a minor player at best. It was hard knowing how to react. Go hard at them with all of your youthful energy and passion, and all you manage to do is stamp yourself as a big-head who has no respect for those who have greater records and reputations, and potentially annoy a powerful figure.

The following scenario would certainly have taken place around Australian cricket.

Cricket powerbroker (maybe coach or selector): 'What about young so and so from X? He's got some real potential—what do you think?'

Powerful player (thinking of their encounter earlier in the season when 'so and so' had been quick on the lip): 'Well, I dunno. I've heard he's a bit lazy and I think there's better than him. What about Y? He was super impressive for us when we played so and so and I know he's got a great temperament and good work ethic.'

The other alternative is to stay in your box and try not to look sideways in case you are perceived as being disrespectful. And that means you are normally seen as being easily intimidated, which ends up with a similar outcome.

Earning respect. It was something that had been drummed into me at Northern Districts, and then reinforced by the likes of Boof, 'Dizzy' Gillespie, 'Blocker' Wilson and coaches like Tim Nielsen and Wayne Phillips. Confidence is a great thing to have when you're starting out, but respect will sustain you in the long term.

I was competitive, and probably came across as confident in that first season and not overawed by the occasion, but it took me a long time to think I really belonged. Deep down I really didn't have the belief that I could do it at that level. I did find myself playing reputations rather than the players in front of me. It was only natural, I guess, to find it tough bowling to Steve and Mark Waugh. I was excited to be up against some greats of the game, but once the excitement stopped bubbling long enough for me to look at the task ahead, inevitably I would find myself wondering if I was good enough to get them out.

Funnily enough, that season's second game against NSW featured a young player who personified precocious—well, certainly as much as the man he would eventually succeed as national captain.

Teenager Michael Clarke made his debut and batted 7 for NSW against the Redbacks at the Adelaide Oval in January 2001. The nickname 'Pup' might not have been in wide circulation at the time, but I'm sure we all thought, 'Oh well, here's another rosy-cheeked Blue bagger who's already got his baggy green', as David Hookes had once professed.

I was probably torn between showing a fellow greenhorn that I had some empathy for the position he was in, and wanting to make sure I finished on top and reinforced the fragile 'status' that my five one-day games to date had earned me. Within two years time he had made his One-Day International (ODI) debut for Australia and his career trajectory was up, up and away. Mine, on the other hand, had been on and off the launch pad without quite getting to orbit.

My second season with the Redbacks was one that probably encapsulated where I was as a cricketer and a person.

I made my first-class debut in a truly amazing game, but also sustained a serious injury that probably set me on a pattern of behaviour that, looking back, I was incredibly fortunate to overcome. I'd had what I thought was a pretty good off-season and preseason. I had been working on my strength in the gym and might have overdone the upper body work as it turned out.

I had to bide my time for the first month, playing a few more one-dayers, but November brought the call I had been waiting for—I was to make my Pura Cup debut for South Australia against Tasmania in Hobart. And even better, it looked like I would share the new ball with Mark Harrity. I was as happy as a dog with two tails, and thought: 'Now this is more like it.'

I was raring to go, and any nerves were quickly dispelled when Boof won the toss and elected to have first use of a Bellerive Oval wicket that either played like a featherbed or a minefield back in those days. Those dreams you have about being an instant success ... that was me that morning. My first scalp was the Tigers number three Michael 'Cowboy' Dighton, followed by Shane Watson—then an emerging but raw talent who had been enticed from his native Queensland to play for Tasmania. And then, four balls into my tenth over, it went from dream to nightmare. With my tail up and striving for that bit of extra, I let one go, only to feel sharp, searing pain across my chest. My pectoral muscle chose that moment to tear, and that was me done for the game. All on my first morning. In hindsight, my focus and emphasis on upper-body work had probably done me in. Whatever I had gained in strength, I'd lost in flexibility. Whatever, I was devastated. I'd waited for the chance, but then blown it by getting hurt and letting down the team.

The usual rule of thumb is that when you lose a frontline member of the attack for the match, it is very hard to win the game, unless someone plays out of their skin. Tassie went from being in strife at 5–122 to powering away to 7–382 off the back of a great 141 from wicketkeeper Sean Clingeleffer and 84 from all-rounder Shaun Young. Mark Harrity bowled 35 overs and Paul Rofe, who had come through with me at youth level, rolled through 44 overs—all while I watched miserably from the sidelines. After getting some treatment across the day, and into the next, I tried tentatively to bat in case I was needed. But I couldn't play any shots due to the pain and I resigned myself to the fact that I was now officially a passenger.

Things looked bleak for us, with opener Jeff Vaughan forced from the field early, and our other opener David Fitzgerald dismissed for 31. I mentioned that you needed someone to do something amazing? Enter Greg Blewett and Boof.

The pair proceeded to produce something extraordinary. A stand of 386 turned the game on its head. Who could sit on the sidelines feeling sorry for themselves when this was unfolding? Boof scored 246 while Blewey hit 163 … Boof was mesmerising. He was in such touch; it was almost as if he was taunting them. He would hit it centimetre-perfect to either side of fielders, and every time the Tigers captain Jamie Cox and the bowlers would move someone, he would hit it to where the fielder had just been. David Saker, the hard-nosed former Victorian fast bowler who would later go on to coach England's bowlers, would bowl and then duck as Boof would pound the ball back straight down the ground. We ended up with 5–589 declared, and then saw a shell-shocked Tigers team rolled for 167 in their second innings, with 'Hags' (Harrity) taking a 5-wicket haul. An outright win by an innings and 40 runs ... if I hadn't been crestfallen at my own fate, it would have been a perfect debut. My prognosis was ordinary—eight weeks out. I managed a return late in the season but was nowhere near my best. The one thing I recalled from the game against the Warriors was the big blond WA quick Brad Williams. He bowled like the wind and showed why there were calls for him to take his talents to a higher level. Again, he bowled quick and moved the ball ... there was a recipe there to adopt but whether I could get the ingredients right was another story.

I had an opportunity to go to the UK again for cricket and took it. I came back determined to make up for lost time. Along the way, though, I was starting to develop some traits that were not ideal if my potential was to be realised.

I had some good cricket in me—2003 was when I won the Bradman Medal as the best grade cricketer. That was a huge honour for the club and I was thrilled at how my cricket for Northern Districts was going. Outsiders, though, noticed that my best efforts would invariably come at that level. When I went up to the Redbacks, I would perform in spurts, almost as if I didn't want to bowl fast and take wickets and lead the attack all of the time ... because then it would become expected of me. It was easier to be back in the pack—doing enough but not leading the way.

On the other hand, over those few seasons when I should have been building towards my peak, I went anywhere but where I was supposed to. Wayne Phillips, our coach, despaired of me on occasions, especially when I was rehabbing from injury.

It almost became easier for me to be injured, or sore, so that if I was, the expectations weren't as great and the work I was doing was enough. I was being challenged by the coaching staff, but I wasn't responding the way they wanted me to. I'd be late for training, not terribly, but five minutes here or there, and would offer up that I had been busy paying bills or doing a job. No matter that I would have had all day to do it. I didn't always communicate clearly with the coach as to how I was fairing either.

I became something of a chore for Flipper. I'd turn up to training and see that I wasn't listed on the board for batting or bowling. And would usually turn my nose up and grizzle.

'Ah Ryan, good of you to join us', Flipper would open proceedings. 'And what are you doing today with us?'

I'd mumble that I was on bowling restrictions but could bat.

'Okay, no bowling, some batting.' And then he would pointedly add me to the board and, having dealt with his problem child, would put aside his exasperation and get on with training.

Being young and probably immature in handling situations like this, I would have more of a whinge later about not getting a go.

Wayne did his best to make me see that if anything was going to change, it had to start with me.

One day I made an appointment to go and see him to work out where I fitted and what his plans were for me. I was a bit head-strong and probably didn't choose my words with much (or any) diplomacy.

He listened. He sighed. And took me over to where some pot plants were standing forlornly in the corner.

'Ryan, those pot plants need watering and a bit of attention. At the moment, that's where you can fit in.'

I was mortified, and embarrassed, and filthy all at once. He had used his quick sense of humour to make a valid point but I didn't quite take it onboard, or in the spirit with which it was intended. As I later found out, my spot on the contract list in those seasons was often the subject of intense discussion. I needed to make it impossible *not* to pick me on the list. Instead, I was giving them reasons not to keep me. It would come down to the sixteenth and seventeenth spots, and serious thought was given as to why I should stay on.

The message was coming my way often enough. At our end-of-season reviews, in the off-season, in the preseason, during the summer. I give Flipper credit—he sat me down and kept reminding me that to go to another level, I needed more.

But enjoying myself seemed easier. I was single, and had enough money and time to do so without too much issue. My mates were having fun growing up and so was I. There was plenty of time spent on getting injury payments—essentially getting paid to recover—and so my motivation was all over the shop.

Around then was when I found myself getting on the drink and having a punt more often than socially. Dad used to have a bet on the horses, but was never a huge punter. I got myself stuck into the pokies.

I'd go to club training on a Thursday night, do a bit there and then have a few beers afterwards. We'd then adjourn to our local and play the pokies and bet on the greyhounds and trots. I was a home owner by then, so I actually had used some of my money wisely. It was a shame about the rest though. I'd win some but lose lots too. There would be times when I would borrow from my mates to get me through until my next pay and sometimes Mum and Dad would help out with the mortgage if I was caught short. I always paid them back, and my mates. I bet at the TAB and, occasionally, with the bookies at the track if we all went to the races, but I never bet on credit. I'd lose $1000 or $1500 on one night, and then a few days later win $4000. I would find myself in debt and in a few tight spots without getting into serious trouble. Fortunately, I was a pretty unsophisticated punter. I never got into betting on sport, certainly not cricket, as the intricacies didn't grab me. Even now, I enjoy playing cards at a casino, and have some interests in owning greyhounds, trotters and racehorses, but I have got to a point where I have my limits and do it for enjoyment and relaxation. Even when I was a young bloke, the prize of owning my own home had been a goal, and that hasn't changed.

Despite my self-inflicted headaches, I had plenty going right for me, or so I thought. I was probably most comfortable on the cricket field, where I had got a bit of a career going with South Australia. I had a loving and supportive family, plenty of good mates, and a bit of financial security. It was all good. Wasn't it?

CHAPTER 8

TAMING THE INNER BOGAN

Greg Blewett has always maintained that once I get the bogan out of me, I will probably do alright for myself. My ex-Redbacks teammate has made his well-dressed way in the world as a television personality and would-be pro golfer since hanging up his boots. And I'm not really able to damn the debonair ex-Test batsman in print for eternity for his opinion … as I concede he might possibly have a point.

Certainly my brother Gavin would not have to think terribly long to dredge up a few examples of my inner bogan coming to life as a young bloke rocking the suburbs after leaving school. While he enjoyed his trips home to see Mum and Dad, the suave Sydneysider, as he was then, also enjoyed appraising his younger brother's fashion sense (limited), hairstyles (spiky) and music (loud).

I was torn between horror and hilarity when the Channel 7 show *Bogan Hunters* nominated Adelaide and 'the

10-kilometre radius around the General Motors factory at Elizabeth' as the source of Australia's best suburban bogans during the show's run in 2014.

Lucky they didn't have a time machine. My first car (complete with pavement-shaking subwoofer), a predilection for blond hair tints and local taverns would have marked me as fair game, along with pretty much everyone else I knew.

It's funny, but you only ever notice the good stuff when you grow up in a certain town or suburb. This selective blindness through rose-coloured glasses usually means it comes as a bit of a rude shock to learn that others see something completely different to you.

But playing footy and cricket does provide you with plenty of opportunities to have your home's shortcomings highlighted to you, and vice versa for the opposition. Anyway, as a number of commentators have suggested in recent times (I think Warney was one of them)—we're all bogans to someone, even you, Blewey.

But we bogans are a resilient bunch. I once heard it said that your twenties are for living and learning—and while I had the living part of it down pat, the learning was a bit harder to marry up. Cricket-wise, though, I was on a well-worn path, trodden by many a wide-eyed youngster as they moved from youth cricket to senior cricket. After missing the under-17 representative scene, I was able to make the South Australian under-19 team two seasons in a row: in 1997–98 and 1998–99.

The 1997 side was a pretty handy one, featuring future Redbacks Graham Manou, Dan Harris, Luke Williams and

Paul Rofe. Former Australian limited-overs bowler Andrew Zesers was our manager/coach. We made the final and played NSW at the Melbourne Cricket Ground. As you'd imagine, that was a big deal for all of us. It is a cavernous ground and when you play there with just a smattering of spectators, it is quite easy to get distracted by the vastness of the place. The other distraction was that for the final, the MCG had its ground broadcast cameras and replay screen in operation. You can imagine how a stack of teenage cricketers coped with that. Blokes were wearing away the turf with the constant turning to check out the replays. The game was a draw but South Australia won on first innings, a big deal for the state. Choc Manou was player of the tournament and, with several of us returning the following year, hopes were certainly high within SA cricket circles about the potential prospects of our crop.

It wasn't quite the same result the following season, though, with SA losing on first innings in the play-off for third place. Michael Klinger was the man who ensured the result with a classy 139 not out for the Vics, and South Australian was certainly pleased he opted to pursue his career in Adelaide with the Redbacks a few years later.

With those experiences, and having played a fair bit of first grade despite my age, it was almost accepted without question that I would go to cricket's equivalent of finishing school and chase the sun away from an Australian winter with a playing stint in England. My English heritage meant that I was pretty easy to place with a club team and with the UK hosting the cricket World Cup in 1999, I was on the big white freedom bird as soon as our season had finished.

A mate of Gavin's had organised for me to join Gerrards Cross in Buckinghamshire, to the north of London. In addition to playing for them, I was employed as a coach with the associated Gerrards Cross Sports Club. I basically tried to replicate a mix of what we used to do at Northern Districts and with the SA under-19s. After my first proper session as coach, I was queried by an incredulous local as to why I had them running around the field for warm-ups. To some of the club supporters, I must have seemed like some cutting edge, New Age coach, albeit with a very fresh face, but all I was doing was trying to imitate what I had experienced myself.

The club had found rooms for me and one of the other overseas players with the club, a young Kiwi named Andy. We rented rooms off a very nice lady named Angela, who was in her forties and lived in Uxbridge. I was still nineteen and tried to make sure I was on my best behaviour when she was around. I did my bit around the place and kept pretty neat and tidy, regularly washed up and the like. We settled in pretty well, although it soon became apparent that, of her two lodgers, she was a bit down on one of them. It wasn't me—although one disastrous incident almost did me in too.

I never really had pets growing up. I had a fish for a while and I remember hearing that Gav had a bird when he was little.

As it turned out, my landlady had a budgie, which she would let out regularly when she was home. It would fly around the room, land on your head or your shoulder, chirrup and sing and generally enjoy its time out of the cage. Gav and his wife Beth had arranged to come over for a holiday, maybe see a World Cup game and visit me. Beth was pregnant at the time with their first child, my nephew Ben, and so we did things together and they travelled and toured a bit before Beth went home, leaving Gav with me for another week or two.

On this particular day, for some reason I wanted to show him the bird and how tame it was. I was keen to show it off for Gav, so I got ready to let it out.

'What about the window there?' Gavin pointed out a tiny gap at the bottom of the window in the kitchen above the sink.

Nah nah nah, it will be fine, I insisted, it flies around here all the time.

So the door opens and like a blue-and-green streak, it was gone. Didn't deviate a centimetre. Straight to freedom through the gap at the bottom, which on second look was big enough to let a parrot through, let alone a thumb-sized budgie. It didn't even look back.

Bugger, bugger, bugger, bugger.

That budgie must have been like those old-time lags in prison, who get through each day by going over every possible escape plan and scenario in their head. I can just imagine how our hardened feathered fugitive might have seen it unfold.

- Dozy duo from down under—check.
- Window over the sink open—check.
- Cage door open—check.
- FREEDOM at last!—check.

Well, we were in a flap. There we were—walking around the yard and then the adjoining park, and then the adjoining streets, doing our best budgie impressions, whistling away, me desperately hoping our missing jail bird was going to find the wide world a bit confronting and come back to a friendly voice.

As those hopes became increasingly forlorn, our thoughts took a logical turn—could we find a replacement for her loving companion before she got home? No. That would last only until she opened the cage up. And new Bluey would either cower in the corner, or make a break for it somewhere else.

In the end, I made a clean breast of it. I wasn't turned out onto the street, although things were a little strained for a while. I was still the favourite lodger.

Even though I had unwittingly reduced the household by one, Angela really couldn't cop our New Zealand guest. We found out what might have been at the source of this when Gav and I came home late one evening not long after the bird had flown the coop.

I had a PlayStation in my room, so were playing games and finishing off a few beers, and, like you do, we started to imitate Andy and speak in rubbish Kiwi accents. I imagine we were probably getting a bit rowdy, which was when Angela suddenly came storming into the room.

It quickly became apparent that 'Andy's' rowdiness had tipped her over the edge and a reckoning was here. She was out for Andy's blood!

'Where is he?' she demanded.

'Who?' we both said, sounding like a startled nest of owls.

'Andy. Where is he? I heard him making all that noise. I want him to be quiet now or that's it.'

Even though we insisted that Andy wasn't around (he had seen the writing on the wall and had been spending less and less time there when Angela was home), she would not believe it.

We took half an hour to convince her that it was the pair of us who were taking the puss (so to speak) …

I think I had to do the vacuuming a bit more after that to calm the troubled waters.

Still, it was a sensational summer. We got to some World Cup games and went to the famous tied semi-final between Australia and South Africa at Edgbaston, in Birmingham. We had a big day and I was a bit unsteady on my pins as the tension began to escalate in those final balls as South Africa dramatically imploded. The clear thinking from Damien Fleming secured the tie and passage to the final. I wasn't as clear at the time, but was certainly caught up in the moment, and jumped the fence with all of the other wild colonial boys, fell over, got back up and charged out to the middle, singled out Boof for a big high-five and a hug before wobbling off towards the exit as security and police tried to get things under control.

After that, we just had to go to the final against Pakistan at Lord's. We managed to get a ticket and enjoyed Australia's comfortable 8-wicket win. My day got even better when I managed to talk my way into the jubilant Aussie rooms.

There I was, the teenage bogan from Adelaide rubbing shoulders with Boof, Warney, the Waugh twins, 'Ooh Ah' Glenn McGrath, Gilly, Punter, Flem ... and drinking their beer and champagne. My luck stayed in, with Boof tucking me under his wing and taking me to the official team party afterwards. I'm pretty sure he put me in a taxi to go home not long after the touring party all got to the celebration bash.

It was a hugely memorable summer on top of my World Cup experience. I played some good cricket and Mum and Dad also came over to visit. I didn't really want the season to end. It was the first of several stints in England. I had three seasons with Lowerhouse in the Lancashire League while I was with South Australia. I was injured in 2003 so only played part of the season, but went back in 2006 and also filled in on another trip. I enjoyed the club and the people there and liked being the paid man; 'the pro', as their supporters would refer to you. The best thing about being the overseas professional is that you can really build your confidence by batting and bowling in a competitive environment each week. The worst thing is that you are expected to do that every week and be successful. I went as a bowler originally but ended up batting the top three and getting some hundreds: all very useful experience ahead of the next Aussie season and one of the reasons why I was able to mount a case for inclusion in the Redbacks' squad as an all-rounder.

Ironically, my last trip to England as a professional was not a success. I didn't get on the field with Sussex in 2007.

I had been wrestling with whether to sign with Queensland after having such a breakthrough season with South Australia. I actually hadn't wanted to stop playing because I had been feeling so good, so it made sense to head back to the UK. The English county system had taken a number of different positions on how to incorporate overseas players and those who qualified through European Union passports and dual passport holders into their structure. The English Cricket Board was working on ensuring that county teams did not go overboard recruiting players who were going to occupy a spot that would have otherwise been filled by an English-qualified player.

Some players who wanted to play in the county system, but didn't necessarily want to qualify for England, had sought legal interpretations under EU laws about whether there was restraint of trade. Players coming over from one season to the next would potentially face a change in the regulatory framework each year.

Through my management, I was keen to keep my earning potential going by playing in England when I could. Even though it looked as if I were going to be accepting an offer from one of the teams who were chasing me back in Australia, I thought I could continue playing in the UK without issue. I was aware there had been changes, though, and soon found myself caught in an awkward spot when I was asked whether I intended to play for Australia or declare myself as an English-qualified player. If that happened, to play state cricket in Australia would mean I would be considered as an international player, and the same argument would apply from Cricket Australia, in that I would potentially take up a spot that could be filled by an Australian player. My simplistic view was that I just wanted to play! So I found myself being not entirely forthcoming to Mike Gatting and the Sussex committee about my intentions. I was aware the landscape had changed, but naively still hoped I could somehow duck all of that and keep my options open. As it was, Queensland had reached an agreement with me. That news broke as I was readying myself for my first game with Sussex. It quickly became apparent that I wasn't going to be getting away with anything. It came down to a decision by the English Cricket Board as to whether they would register me and allow me to take the field. They wouldn't and I didn't. I was standing with the CEO and coach on the sideline as the Sussex captain Chris Adams was about to toss when the word came through. So that was that. After some awkward discussions, I made plans and two days later flew home to what, hopefully, would be a new future.

CHAPTER 9

OWN WORST ENEMY

'Hey. Hey! Wake up. WAKE UP!'

Someone was shaking my foot. What the …

My eyes finally opened to see a bloke standing at the end of my bed. Who the hell was he and what was he doing in my room?

'C'mon get up.'

My eyes were still focussing, my head was fuzzy and still catching up with what was going on. What *was* going on?

'I'm a detective with the Northern Territory police. There's been a sexual complaint.'

What the … Did I hear that right? Is he saying rape?

What is he talking about? A complaint?

'You're kidding me,' I finally rasped something out.

'It's no joke. Get UP NOW!'

Okay, okay. I'm up, putting clothes on. I can hear someone else in the apartment. Rowan. He's blowing up deluxe.

'This is BULLSHIT!'

I seek him out. Righto, calm down Brewy. We'll get to the bottom of this. We haven't done anything. You've done nothing wrong, I've done nothing wrong ...

And now I hear things a lot more clearly. My head suddenly isn't that fuzzy. The hangover sweat is icy on my forehead. My guts are churning for real.

A complaint of sexual assault! If it wasn't dry beforehand, I've got a serious case of cotton mouth now.

I can see in the corner of my eye the towering trellis that is Peter George. He looks bewildered and a bit scared. Someone is talking to him, there are khaki uniforms and some blokes in plain clothes who look in charge.

An explanation is taking place ... they're not just popping in. I hear them talking about going to the station and I know it's not to catch a train.

'Do we need to cuff you?' Someone with authority in his voice asks me.

'Mate, I'm not going to run anywhere. I'll come and tell you what happened. But we have to get a flight in a few hours.'

Nuh uh. We weren't going to be getting on a flight anytime soon.

My thinking was catching up to the gravity of the situation now. We had to tell someone. The Redbacks coach Wayne Phillips was in charge of the squad and word was got to him.

Flipper got to the nitty-gritty quickly. Did we do anything wrong? I swore I hadn't. It was a mistake. It had to be. Okay,

Flipper was onto it. Someone would get to the bottom of this for us, surely?

As preparations were made for our squad to go home, minus the three of us, the room was being searched. It was a crime scene as far as the authorities were concerned.

And so there we were. In the Darwin watch house at a time when most people were settling down to breakfast.

It was all a long, long way from having a few beers after winning a cricket match.

It was 2005 and I was in Darwin with the South Australian squad at the annual winter Academies Challenge, which brought teams from each of the states and the centre of excellence together for some preseason matches.

We hadn't enjoyed the best of trips on the field, but had finished with a win in our last game and were enjoying our last night.

I was contracted to the SACA then and was rooming with Rowan Brewster, a left-handed batsman from NSW who had come to Adelaide in a bid to crack first-class cricket after performing at youth and second XI level and going to the Cricket Academy.

I was twenty-five and Rowan was twenty-four. We got on alright, as teammates tend to do, even if it was a relatively short-term acquaintance. The other roomie was an up-and-coming young cricketer, who was quiet, shy and cautiously making his way in the world. Definitely not a party animal.

It had been a good night, but not an out-of-control evening. We went out as a group and came back pretty much together.

At some point, Rowan had met a girl and she had come back to the apartment too. It was late, and our collective decision-making was not at its clearest, but as I maintained from the outset, nothing happened that I believed was wrong.

If anything, I was confident that just telling the truth would clear things up. I hadn't done anything *wrong*. Surely that was all it would take?

So what was going on a few hours later now that we had a room full of police? Instead of the usual mad scramble to pack, get some water into us and be downstairs in time to get to the airport for the morning flight home, we were all told in no uncertain terms that this was serious.

Questioning at the watch house took place for a few hours. There was a rape squad detective and the original detective who had woken me.

That went on for a while. They were direct, and left out no detail from the allegations. I told them what had happened—and didn't waver from what I had said, even if it was different from what they were trying to suggest might have happened. The others were elsewhere.

Afterwards, we waited. Separate cells. A rubber bench, a toilet bowl in the corner, glass door. Bare walls, strange, disconcerting sounds. It was clean, like it had been cleaned every day, as if the presence of the last person who had occupied the same space had been clinically washed away once they had been moved on to whatever fate awaited them next.

Your imagination goes nuts. I was worrying about getting to Mum and Dad and telling them what was going on. Shit.

Dad was supposed to pick me up at the airport … I hope someone has rung them.

One of the policemen who had driven us to the watch house came by. He had seemed a reasonable bloke and I asked what was happening.

Not long now, he assured. Just checking a few more things. Looking pretty good though. An hour later he came back.

Ah no. Not good, not good at all. Rowan and I were going to be charged with sexual intercourse without consent and aggravated assault. Our other young roomie had assisted with inquiries, and was going to be released.

Another blur of cell doors opening and closing, standing in front of some mildly indifferent police officers, for photographs and then fingerprints. It was like television on the surface but underneath, there were no illusions. It was horribly real. We were bailed, and eventually released. It was evening, and the three of us went back to the hotel, shell-shocked, stunned and scared.

I finally got to talk to Dad and told him that we had done nothing wrong. He listened but really just wanted to get me home. At the hotel, we went over the past twenty-four hours. We were still very shaken at how matters had spiralled into a position we would not have dreamed of finding ourselves in.

Both Rowan and I had stuck to our original position and by the sound of it, our accounts matched up. But that didn't matter. It was a matter of record now, the media had been informed, and word was quickly sweeping around Adelaide and other cricket circles.

Somehow I got a few hours' sleep and was up to catch the same flight that we had been scheduled to catch the day before. We reached Adelaide and were quickly hustled out a side door and whisked away to an urgent meeting with SACA Chief Executive Officer, Mike Deare, and other senior staff and their legal advisor.

At the SACA, our young roomie's mum and dad and girlfriend were there. They looked more distressed than him. I went over and apologised that he had found himself involved and assured them he was fine. He had done nothing wrong. We had done nothing wrong. It was becoming a mantra.

The SACA were good. They listened, asked questions and began to work on some plans. There was support for us and for our families, which I was immensely grateful for.

There was plenty of media interest in the case and, as the only SACA contracted player, I was probably the focus of it. One thing that buoyed my spirits was that the vast majority of people backed me and believed me. No-one sledged me on the field about it, at the time or since.

The case was taken to the NT Director of Public Prosecutions. After several weeks of waiting, we got the nod. Charges dropped. I was at a preseason camp in Mildura with the Redbacks when I was tracked down with the news.

There was immense relief, but also some anger. I got cranky when the SACA wanted to issue a statement immediately, when I wanted to come back to Adelaide to speak in person to the media the next day. I was overruled and, with my emotions running high, perhaps that might have been a sensible call. But it didn't make me any less upset.

Our legal team told us afterwards there had been threats made against us during and after the period when we were waiting to learn our fate. Apparently someone close to the complainant had a gun and was keen to show us if we came back to Darwin.

I know now that there are no winners in a case like this. I don't know what happened to the girl who lodged the complaint, nor did I ever find out what compelled her to go to the police.

I was single at the time and I took a long time to trust people again. I didn't go out in public for a fair while—I'd stay in, or go to a mate's place, but not out.

One of the first times I went out with a girl again afterwards, I toyed with asking her whether she would agree to let me record her on my phone … saying she was going out with me of her own accord. Not really a conventional way to start a first date off, and an idea I abandoned quickly as being just too weird.

I did agonise about raking this all up again, even if it is a matter of public record. I hate talking about it, my wife Cherie hates it being brought up, and there will be members of our families who were blissfully unaware of any of this until now.

It was over and done with and in the pasts of all concerned. All I can offer is that telling this is part of my story, for better or worse, and I would not have been true to myself had I simply pretended it happened to another Ryan Harris, and this chapter never saw the light of day. I had a few flashbacks when Leader of the Opposition Bill Shorten addressed a historic complaint against him of a similar nature during 2014. One thing that he said during the coverage resonated with me: 'That's not who I am.' I would offer the same response to anyone who wanted to revisit things in my case.

Each of us moved on. Rowan ended up moving to Brisbane a few years after I did, and played first grade with one of the Brisbane clubs. We'd caught up a few times briefly, but you can understand that we found other things to talk about than those days.

If there is a message I would offer to aspiring athletes, it is to always remember that ultimately, you are responsible for the situation you put yourself in. Set yourself a standard of conduct and stick to it. It might sound hypocritical coming from someone who learned the hard way but, knowing what I know now, you would rather not have the regret of wishing you could go back in time and make a different decision.

I made one other trip to Darwin after that, as coach with Australia A in a quad series during the winter of 2014. It was strange. I'd been apprehensive when we first arrived after getting my thoughts down about the original incident and reliving those days while writing this book.

I wasn't nervous that anything bad was going to happen, just out of kilter. I recognised a lot of the places, and I found myself one day going past the watch house and trying to recall where we were taken. After a few days, that feeling of being ill at ease faded and I found Darwin a better spot than I remembered—maybe my older, wiser self, was more prepared to move on than I realised.

The term 'wake-up call' is a bit of a misnomer, because you don't necessarily wake up to yourself straight away. But Darwin was one of those incidents that did change me, if only to remind me firmly that I still had an opportunity to make something of myself, as long as I could concentrate on cricket. After all, as a twenty-five-year-old with some strikes against me, the alarm bells would already have been ringing in cricket circles. Or even worse, I had already been considered and discarded without my knowledge. If that had happened my chance was gone already.

But as it turned out, my eyes might have been opened wider, but I still had more waking up to do.

CHAPTER 10

A SIMPLE GESTURE

It's a simple gesture. Sometimes it is over and done before I even realise I have done it. But the quick touch of a new ball to my heart when I am about to bowl for Australia means the world to me. It's that fleeting moment when I think: 'Okay Mum, here I am again. Time to do my best. I hope I make you proud.'

And then I'm away. Running the steps back to reality and the job at hand.

Among my fondest memories of my mum are the ones that have her smiling. It usually revolved around her enjoying the social life that naturally comes with being a part of a club or organisation that you get involved with.

A lot of the constants when I was coming along playing junior cricket and in the grades with Salisbury and Northern Districts were of Mum and Dad watching while I played. Mum having a few Grant Burges after the end of a day's play at the club house, having a laugh and chatting with Dad and the club stalwarts like Bruce Jolly and her mates and Dad driving us home later on, all tired but happy. Mum worked for Qantas and had lots of friends around the place, so she was never short of someone to catch up with. I always thought of her as the smiling, laughing one, who would be quick to cheer and celebrate when something went right, and just as quick to spark you up if it didn't go to plan.

She loved to support Gav and me. In my early days of playing for the Redbacks, when our matches took place on weekdays, she would find a way to duck away from work, either an early or late lunch, or finish a bit early to come down to the Adelaide Oval and watch the last hour or so of play. Often she would be there at stumps, and I'd look up and spot her.

The 2005–06 season was coming to an end and I was getting ready to follow the well-worn off-season path to England blazed by me and other up-and-comers. I was looking forward to heading back over for another northern summer, catching up with some old mates, and playing some League cricket with Lowerhouse in between enjoying the best of what England and Europe had to offer.

Mum had been complaining of being a little short of breath. She'd been a smoker for most of her adult life and that wasn't something that bothered me in the slightest. It was just something that was part of her make-up and the ignorance of childhood and youth ensured I didn't dwell on what that might mean for her, or us. For her to complain though … she had always been the type to soldier on and not let us know if she was crook.

But this must have been troubling her and a visit to the doctor in early April 2006 set alarm bells ringing. It all happened quickly, with the bad news coming like a boxer throwing knockout punches against a hapless opponent caught in the corner. Suspected lung cancer, confirmed lung cancer, a trip to an oncologist followed by chemotherapy, all in rapid succession and a few weeks before I was supposed to be on a plane. Once we had dealt with the shock, we tried to rationalise what was going to happen.

The medical opinion had been guarded, but there was optimism of sorts. Aggressive treatment was prescribed and Mum and Dad were putting on a positive front. I went along with that, but in my lone moments, I thought about how helpless I felt and what I could possibly do for her.

My first reaction was that I wasn't going to England. How could I? But Mum was very calm and insistent. She was feeling well, the treatment had started and she had taken a lot of resolve from how everyone had handled things. She hadn't wanted to tell the world, and so it was only a relatively small circle of family and friends who she turned to with the news. So reluctantly, but with a sense of relief that maybe things were going to work out, I got on a plane and flew off with a packed cricket kit and just as many fears, worries and hopes in my head to keep me occupied for the hours, days and weeks ahead.

I grew to both dread and anticipate our regular chats on the phone. As much as I tried to glean how she was doing

Above: At primary school, thinking about the next break and what game I am going to play, I suspect.

Right: Ready for action at my nan's home at Elizabeth North.

Above: One of the legendary family backyard games at my nan's place that produced tears and triumph on an annual basis.

Below left: With my cousins, (left to right) me, Michael and Russell, playing for Elizabeth Downs. Soccer was one of my early loves. *Below right*: Indoor cricket was perfect for me, and you got to wear sleeveless shirts. I'm in the centre at the front.

Left: Dad, Mum, Gavin (arriving at a bad shirt party that only he was aware of) and me, all dressed up with somewhere to go.

Below left: Me with my first set of clubs. Golf's wonderful fun but I am very glad I chose the sport I did!

Below right: At Trinity College, sporting one of my better haircuts.

Above: Mum (in blue) with her friends Sue Boettcher and Iris Prust.

Right: Dad and I, just before my one-day debut for South Australia, in the famous pergola.

Above: A nest of Redbacks – look hard and you can spot Boof Lehmann, Dizzy Gillespie and a very blond Mark Cosgrove.

Below: Getting the prized Redbacks signature bats done, with (left to right) Andy Delmont, Dr Dan Harris and I.

Above: The South Australia Cricket squad at the Adelaide Oval in 2005-06.

Below: My 21st birthday, where Boof and Blewey (Greg Blewett) had just told me the news that I would be making my debut for the Redbacks. Do I look happy enough!

Right: In full cry for SA in a Mercantile Mutual Cup game against the Vics in 2000, at the old-school surrounds of Punt Road rather than the MCG.

Below: Close, but not close enough as Brad Haddin takes the bails off to run me out in a one-dayer in 2004 at Manuka Oval in Canberra. Shame the third umpire couldn't save me!

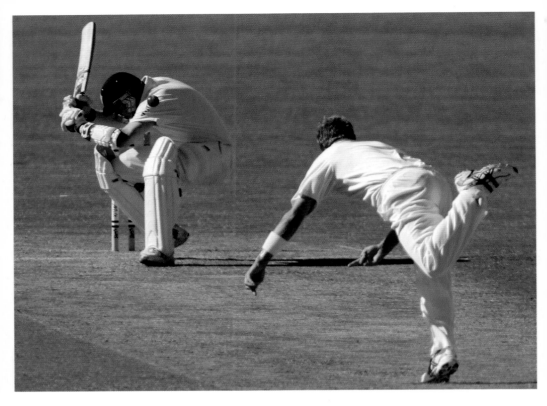

Above: Bouncing Grant Lambert, the NSW all-rounder who was inevitably a thorn in our sides, at the Adelaide Oval in 2007–08, my last season with the Redbacks before moving to Queensland.

Right: On the charge with the Queensland Bulls in a Twenty20 game at the Gabba, a young Aaron Finch in the background and former Test paceman cum umpire Paul Reiffel giving me some good news.

from the tone of her voice, whether she was catching her breath, if she sounded strained or tired ... she sounded just like the Mum I left. My secret fear was that I would talk to her one day and something would happen and I wouldn't hear from her again.

I didn't think I was a mummy's boy, but as a family we were very close. I remember that on the occasions when I was a young bloke going away for a rep carnival somewhere like Mount Gambier or Kingston where we would be billeted out with local families, I didn't do that well. There would be instant homesickness as soon as I got to where I was supposed to be, and usually a couple of tears that first night. But on the end of a phone line, Mum did a very good job of keeping things on an even keel, as she would continue to do.

Mum would tell me early on in our conversation that treatment had been going well. She might admit to being a bit 'tired' but inevitably it was upbeat. Gav and I would compare notes sometimes, and we'd come to the conclusion that maybe she was getting better. The cricket in England was going okay, and I was living the usual lifestyle of an 'overseas pro' in League, which usually revolved around some coaching during the week, perhaps some 'sub pro' experience as a fill-in player for another team in another League and then batting and bowling to win each weekend. The rusted-on fans of your club would inevitably have an opinion after the first week as to whether you were a 'good 'un' and if you were, then nothing was too much of a problem. Being a returning player meant I was already on their good side, and I was very fortunate that there was always a sympathetic ear or a friendly face around if I needed a pick-up during those times when I was worrying about Mum.

Things did seem to be working out as well as could be expected for Mum. She finished her course of chemotherapy and again, everyone seemed positive enough. She was feeling well so she and Dad decided to take a short holiday to Phuket in Thailand. Unfortunately, after only a short period of rest and relaxation, she started to feel unwell again. When they got home, it was back to the specialists and the indication that the cancer had reappeared. So off they went to tackle it again. But Mum's brave face with me was starting to be a challenge. She rang Gav shortly after it had been diagnosed again and it finally cracked.

'I thought I was getting better. I was getting better and now I've been told that I am not. What are we going to do?' It was a question that Gav had to battle to answer—I wouldn't have got a word out if it had been me on the other end of the line.

It was August soon enough and as Lowerhouse weren't going to win the league, they generously suggested I go home early to be with Mum. It was a long flight home ... I got back to Adelaide on the morning she was having her last treatment of the current course of chemo. I spent the day with her at the hospital, snatching some sleep in a chair beside her when jet lag intervened, and otherwise catching up and spending time together. I didn't know what to expect when I saw her again, but aside from looking a bit more strained and tired, she was the mother I knew and loved.

Mum came through the last lot of treatment and again, seemed positive about the next steps. She was tired a lot, but we were still able to do some of the usual things we did as a family. Club cricket had started and Mum and Dad would come along to watch me and catch up with friends as they normally did. I hit one of my highest scores of 168 in those early rounds, the last time she saw me bat as it turned out.

As we had done more times than we could remember, the family shared something special together over a game of cricket a few weeks before she died. Gav had been spending some time over with us when he could, and on that particular Saturday when Northern were playing East Torrens, Mum had her last chance to see both of us on the field together. Gav had come down and was about to grab a beer from the bar when one of our fielders injured himself early on. Boof was playing and he promptly seconded Gav to borrow some whites and get on the field as our substitute fielder. He ended up in the field for a couple of hours and we had a great arvo out there together, with Mum and Dad watching like old times from the sideline. Gav chimed in with a run-out off Boof's bowling as well, so you can imagine the fun that was had in the dressing-room afterwards. The sun was setting and we were both hot, pretty tired but happy. Boof was roaming around handing out cold beers and rubbishing us, reliving Gav's 'golden arm', and generally making merry. Mum and Dad enjoyed the post-play laughs and all was as it had been, and should have been for years to come.

Instead, a few weeks later, she was gone.

Despite her ongoing stoicism, Mum was feeling unwell again and, even though she was between treatments, went to the hospital one Sunday. They checked her in, and decided to keep her in for a few days to run some more tests and map out what treatment or palliative care they should explore. She was in good spirits on the Tuesday and enjoyed her visitors so we weren't expecting what happened next.

On the Wednesday, Dad was out picking up a few things to take back to the hospital when he got the call. Mum had taken a turn for the worse. Get here now. We contacted Gav in Sydney and he dropped everything to get on the next plane, and then tried to get as many of the people that Dad and Mum had told.

She hung on until after Gav had arrived. We were at her bedside when she slipped away close to midnight. There's a blur then of tears and sadness. Plenty of hugs, and later, when things needed to be taken care of, encouraging pats on the back and arms around shoulders.

There is a strange numbness that can strike you in such circumstances, and I was numb alright. Even though I had imagined something like this happening when the unknown was all I had to fear, it was just so hard to deal with.

Somehow we got through the next few days—some of Mum's friends were terribly shocked, as they had been reassured by her confident front and were not prepared at all for the fact that she had been dying without them knowing. Gav and I and Dad tried to comfort where we could but it wasn't easy. At some point during those days, someone mentioned cricket to me. Was I going to play for Northern on the weekend?

I probably bit their head off—no! No way. Who could think of cricket at a time like this? I know I couldn't.

But wiser heads than me persisted. Gently at first, then with a little more pushing. I think it was thrashed out over a bottle or two of scotch as we all dealt with our loss, and I was nudged towards changing my view.

Dad and Gav both recall telling me that Mum would have wanted me to play, *expected* me to play. And so I did. It was a weekend round—Saturday and Sunday—and there was a bigger than usual crowd at the ground. Mum and Dad's friends, family, friends of Gav and I, work colleagues of Mum, all turned up to pay their respects. I was emotional, but as it happens when I get onto the field and get involved in the game, everything melted away and I simply played what was in front of me. Powerful emotions—sorrow, anger, regret, love—fuelled me that game. I bowled quick, consistently quick, and the ball went where it was supposed to. At the end of the game, I had 14 wickets to my name, 7 in each innings, and part of me was ready to move on to the week ahead when we would bury Mum and say our final farewells.

Gav did the eulogy—a mighty effort—as I knew I wouldn't have been up to it. My most challenging task had been to provide a formal identification at the funeral home. But once that had been done, Dad and I took Gavin's young kids, Ben and Lilly, in so they could see their granny one last time. We slowly began to get on with things in the days and weeks after the service.

Even though I had some success that round immediately after Mum's passing, cricket didn't have a lock on me or my emotions after that. The game was poorer for me without her. I mulled over whether I should have a break from the game. Why not? I didn't seem to be going anywhere in a hurry. When I'd go down that path, I'd get angry and almost convince myself that the last thing I should be doing was playing cricket. And at some point I'd catch myself and go: 'Well, what sort of things were you planning on doing instead?' And I'd see Dad and realise that he was missing Mum too, and Gav and his family were missing her, and that the best thing I could do was keep on with one of the things that knitted us together as a family.

It didn't just click overnight, but after a time, a few things began to go my way as the summer days lengthened.

My season after Mum died had a few moments, but I battled another knee injury early in the summer and there were some deep dips in my motivation during a challenging summer for the SACA. My personal sorrow was one thing, but the longer the 2006–07 season went on, the harder it got for anyone associated with the Redbacks. They won just the one Pura Cup game, the last of the season, where I was able to end the summer on something of a high with a career best, 5–92, in my sixteenth first-class match. At the end of the season, Wayne Phillips stood down as coach and Boof resigned as captain, ensuring our next season would virtually begin from scratch with rookie leaders and coaching staff. I felt for both blokes, on a team and individual level—Flipper had tried his hardest to get something resembling the best out of me, and in spite of my efforts while Boof was the skipper I had always looked up to him. The SACA's appointment of Mark Sorrell as coach was some consolation as I had always found him a good bloke and someone I considered would work around the clock to get things heading in a positive direction. Nathan Adcock, an intelligent and thoughtful cricketer who worked as a lawyer, was identified as a unifying leader and awarded the captaincy.

As for me, I retained my contract during the off-season, although I had the distinct impression that my playing career had only gained a temporary extension rather than a more permanent look. We grieved again on the first anniversary of Mum's death, but as had been the case twelve months earlier, my distraction and saviour was to get back playing. And the green shoots of performance that had sprouted late in 2006–07 gained a little more encouragement as the 2007–08 Pura Cup began to take on new life.

That summer was one to savour, at last. My body was holding together well, my pace was up and the ball was swinging and moving in the areas where I wanted it to go. The fresh start that we craved at the SACA, though, was not as forthcoming.

We lost our first game against the Victorian Bushrangers (a young gun called Peter Siddle, with zinc-painted lips and tinted 'Warney' tips in his hair, ran through us). We lost the next game too, against the Tigers in Hobart after we rolled the dice and declared to set Tassie a second innings run chase following one of the great individual knocks of 190 by Choc Manou that gave us a sniff. But Ricky Ponting (who had hit 96 in their first dig) motored to a match-winning 124 not out as the home side chased down 4–349. You might detect a theme here when I mention we lost our third game outright as well, and while I yearned to sing the team song in a winning dressing-room as much as the next Redback, the fact I had got three games in a row and taken a few wickets in each was secretly keeping me pretty upbeat.

It took a trip to Queensland to break our shaky early-season form, and we took six points off the Bulls at the Gabba in some picture-perfect conditions for fast bowling. The game went just three days, as the mercurial and genuinely frightening Shaun Tait had one of those moments where it all fell into place. He took 7–29 in the Queensland second innings and bowled like a wild wind. I was able to pick up 2–19 as well, and while not going close to Taity in terms of pace, I was thrilled with how I went at the Gabba. We didn't follow up in our next game against the Warriors at another fast bowler–friendly pitch in Perth, but 4–77 from 28 overs was again a personal fillip, with my body getting used to the workload of a first-class bowler. Our return clash with the Vics at Junction Oval saw the one-time axeman Peter Siddle again chop into our batting line-up for a 6-wicket haul, and while we picked up first innings points, the SACA season was again looking fairly shaky heading into the second half of the summer.

Things didn't pick up terribly for the team when Tasmania made the trip to Adelaide, and I found myself in that awkward position of being pleased with my own form but part of a group collectively worrying about where our next win would come from. A career best 7–108 in the first innings of a drawn match put a spring in my stride coming into the next encounter after finishing with nine from the match.

I had already noted the blueprint of Tasmanian quick Ben Hilfenhaus, a strongly built pace bowler who swung it a bit and who had already played ODIs for Australia after a bumper harvest of Shield wickets in 2006–07. We had similar styles, and in the back of my mind I squirreled away the thought that the national selectors liked to pick fast bowlers who swing the ball.

Playing Shield cricket can be a weird experience. You play for sheep stations (and careers) in front of almost empty stadiums in some cities. There can be smatterings of diehard cricket lovers and casual onlookers, members, hardy corporate supporters, some media, security, groundsmen, venue and cricket staff, all dotted around the place. It can be equal parts sleepy and utterly engrossing. We were always pretty fortunate in Adelaide with appreciative members creating just the right amount of buzz. But the excitement is there in the middle—the games mean a hell of a lot to the players and, with careers and livelihoods at stake, they approach their ten first-class games a season as if a Test berth was just around the corner. It can be a slow burn sometimes, but the ebb and flow of the game at Shield level is what makes the game the tough taskmaster that it is. A batsman who can't bat for more than a session will soon find out that others will be favoured. A bowler who rips and tears like a lion in his first outing of the day, and timidly rolls in like a well-fed tabby cat in his last spell, will be found out. The cricket grapevine can disseminate a weakness to others in the game faster than any online gossip site. You learn a lot during those matches, and you are prepared to pay the price to make sure that if a chance does come, you have done what you could to be in the right place.

I'd like to tell you that our final two games of the season were among those experiences where everything clicked for us and we finished on a high. But the scorecards don't lie ... Queensland came down to Adelaide for their return clash and beat us outright to clinch their first win of the season, a similar tale to what we had undergone the season before.

In what also seems a recurring note during the season, I found another career best to add to my short highlights reel, this time with the bat. A 55 not out in our first innings, where the bowlers like Mark Cleary and Dan Cullen and I got us past 200, looked useful on paper. Unfortunately it didn't end up helping the team greatly as the Bulls put us to the sword, thanks to 190 from Shane Watson, who was increasingly stepping up to show his class in that season. The NSW Blues then completed a season to forget for the SACA, with an outright win inside three days at the SCG.

There were one-day games in there as well, and playing regularly alongside blokes like 'Dizzy' Gillespie and Boof as well was adding volumes to my personal databanks. The Redbacks finished third in the one-dayers that season and I played nine games there. But the numbers were starting to stack up for me and ten Shield matches and nine one-dayers was easily the most I had played in a season. The other numbers looked good too—27 first-class wickets at 29.86 and 24.20 with the bat.

But the South Australian scene remained unsettled. Shaun Tait bravely stepped down from cricket to deal with something not a lot of players had considered at the time, the malady of depression, while Boof and Dizzy decided it was time to call it quits on their playing days with the Redbacks. That was a watershed summer in some ways, with similar career decisions that would soon impact on me rippling through other states.

Along the way, I made the decision to get a tattoo—not that I needed a reminder as I thought of Mum every day—but so I could keep her close. So hidden away under my playing shirt whenever I walk on the field is the word 'Mum' and the symbol of her star sign, Virgo. I have very few tattoos on me, her name on my chest and the Southern Cross on my arm, and they are all tied up with achieving Mum's dreams and my own. She never saw me in my baggy green, and so whenever I wear it, I like to think she's with me in some way.

When I played my first Test at the Adelaide Oval against India a few years later, I had friends and family galore around and it was a celebration as much as a memorial to Mum. I found myself looking around as I getting ready to bowl for the first time and remembering how Mum would dart away from the office if she knew I was having a bowl, just to watch an over or two. There was an empty seat somewhere at the Oval that day.

Touching a ball to my heart. It's only a small gesture, but it means the world to me.

CHAPTER 11

BOOF

Where do I start with Darren Lehmann?

Who is he? A caring father figure, a cricketing big brother, the cheeky fun-loving younger brother, a much-admired teacher, your larrikin next-door neighbour, a lover of tradition, a bold innovator, an anti-authoritarian stirrer?

In my experience, he's all of that, and a bit more.

If I was asked to nominate the single most influential person on my career (and there have been a few who have helped, guided, taught, nurtured, scolded and cajoled me along the way), it would be Darren Lehmann. Northern Districts, South Australia, Queensland and Australia ... my career has been intertwined with his for a vast majority of my time.

And it would be as much for the things away from the cricket field as on them that would be the reason why. He showed me how to conduct myself and he pulled me up when I needed it (and if truth be known, he still does pull me up, for instance, when my impulsiveness rears its head or I lose sight of the good things I have).

As a spiky-haired skinny kid making my way in the grades with Northern Districts, my steep learning curve would always get a little sharper when Boof was on our team during one of those windows when he wasn't playing for South Australia or Australia. He had a presence, but most of the time, he would be acting like he was just one of the boys. He'd park himself in slips, do a bit of talking and directing of fielders, and just observe. Us, them, the umpires, the crowd … it all seemed to get fed into his brain, processed, and then somewhere along the way, magic would happen.

You always feel you are with the smartest kid in the room when you watch cricket with Boof. I spent some time on the sidelines with him when he was coaching the Queensland Bulls and Brisbane Heat. I was recovering during the second year of the KFC T20 Big Bash League and he encouraged me to put some training wheels on and have a dabble at coaching. Sitting alongside him for extended periods during a match was like watching an event that was on a time delay.

He would look at a scenario and outline a possible outcome, with his arms folded, swinging animatedly back and forth between the action in the middle and the sideline, chewing gum and running through how it could go.

'I reckon Hopesy [James Hopes] should burn an over from Lynny [Chris Lynn] next over. X likes to hit from the opposite end, but this is the shorter boundary and he will want to get another good over in, so we might tempt him to change his game plan. Lynny will slide the ball into his pads. He might even get him playing over it, or one to stop and grip a bit and maybe get one off his pads back onto the stumps.'

A few moments later, as it all played out, you would take a moment from the jubilation of seeing a key opposition on his way back to the dugouts to marvel at how he had called it. Of course, he would then advance another scenario so outrageous that it couldn't possibly happen, and usually that would be the case. But the dice were always rolling in his head.

He has always been generous with his advice and quick to impart simple pieces of knowledge that make a difference. That is why he was such a good teacher of rookies when he was playing, and why he has been a success the further up the coaching ladder he has gone.

I remember a team meeting for the Heat where one of the discussions was how to play Muttiah Muralitharan, who was playing for the Melbourne Renegades in the BBL—not the easiest bloke in the world to read out of the hand or off the pitch and, even though he was getting close to the end of his career, he was still a formidable prospect. At least one of the young Heat batsmen confessed he had not the slightest clue as to how he was going to approach batting when he got there.

Boof allayed his fears with a few simple bits of advice. 'Mate, look at the first ball, if you can't read it from the hands, get nice and forward outside the line and sweep him. When you can't read him, do that. And don't worry about hitting boundaries. He worries about conceding singles for some reason, so pick those up and you'll find he will bowl quicker and flatter. Then you can slog him and get some runs off him in his last over.'

And that's pretty much how it went when the youngster got to Etihad Stadium. He swept the first ball (with Boof giggling away on the sideline to himself), then nudged a few around for safe singles. After sticking to that simple plan, he then managed to 'slog' a few much-needed boundaries in the Sri Lankan legend's final over.

Of course, Boof was one of those batsmen who could play most bowlers with a matchstick, or at least half a bat. His eye, natural skill and technique were all his, but his assessment of bowlers and batsmen was clinical and could be rolled out to those fortunate enough to be on his side.

It would irritate him when one of his charges would agree to a plan, go out and suddenly revert to what they had agreed he wouldn't do. When that inevitably ended in a dismissal or an opposition batsman getting on top of a bowler, Boof would get the down-turned mouth, maybe dart away for a hasty cigarette, hop on his exercise bike, and think about how he would communicate both his displeasure and the next steps he and the player would take together to ensure it wouldn't happen again.

Then there is his almost unrealistic belief in winning games from seemingly impossible positions. I've heard him speak several times about the influence of the late David Hookes on his way of thinking, and it was that same cavalier, devil-may-care, balls-out approach that Boof would have driving him. As a player, he conjured up remarkable wins for teams he was part of, either through his own efforts or by giving a potential match-winner the licence to create mayhem.

One of my most enjoyable team victories came when Queensland, against all odds, won a final-ball thriller against Victoria at the MCG in the decider of the Ryobi Cup in 2012–13. I was part way through a comeback that had started a week or so earlier in the last regular season one-day game and would continue into a Sheffield Shield final against Tasmania a few weeks later.

Even in the frantic final few balls, where we picked up 2 wickets in 2 balls to win in drizzling rain, Boof was convincing everyone around him that we were going to triumph. I could see him on the sidelines of the MCG, moving about and urging us on. His willpower and belief were such that we all thought it was possible, and when we pinched a win against the odds, he celebrated as hard as the rest of us.

Boof's mantra is pretty straight-forward. You should play to take the game forward; be positive when the tendency might be to go conservative, and not be afraid to lose. The freedom was there to be unorthodox, to try something that the opposition might not be expecting, especially if they were on top. An over of off spin from a fast bowler, use a part-time leg-spinner for an over, rotate your bowling attack through single-over spells, put a fielder in a weird spot, move a batsman up or down the order … anything you can to unsettle the opposition or at least get them to think about what you are doing rather than what they are currently up to.

With Australia, he is well planned, and usually gives us all some simple tasks or KPIs to look at. He likes to break the game down on the white board to sessions, and will tick and cross as we go. By the end of the game, if you have lost, then it is normally pretty simple to see where the game was decided. And if you have won, you know the areas you might exploit next time, and where you might want to improve. He wants you to be relaxed, so outwardly he treats pressure situations as just another game. 'It's just a game of cricket mate', he will tell you, almost willing you to see it as if you were back playing where you were most comfortable, club cricket or for your state. He knows that people can be scared, can fear failure, and doubt themselves or others when they find themselves facing a challenging situation. He will often tell the players about how many times he thought he was out of his depth, and how nervous he was, and it helps them understand that everyone goes through those emotions.

It is something I reckon he got from Hookesy. He was a legend of the game in South Australia, but I never really had much to do with him on a personal level. In fact, the first time I really sat down and heard him speak was earlier on the day he died. I hadn't stayed at the hotel where it all happened, and only found out the next morning when I woke up. It changed Boof as only tragedy can, and his approach to life and cricket changed with him.

As a coach, Boof is relaxed but organised. He likes to prepare things a fair way out, but is flexible enough to make changes if he thinks a better option has presented itself. He preaches family first … you have responsibilities to the team but they are not designed to be mutually exclusive to your family. It is a trust thing—you would never dare to abuse it.

One thing you learn from the outset is that he hates lateness. The Bulls and Heat would regularly present themselves in foyers well before check-out time and the team would inevitably be all ready to leave before the agreed-upon time. To that end, Boof loves a team fines system. It takes on a life and structure all of its own—there is a lot of fun involved but you know that if you are late, then it will need to be one hell of an excuse. And the further he has gone, the bigger the fines have got.

'What are you blokes complaining about, you've all got plenty. Pay up or it's another fine.'

Of course the collected revenue will end up going back to the team in the shape of a social outing, or to charity.

Boof enjoys the fun of being in a team. Somewhere in there, he's still a big kid at heart.

He's done some great stunts in his time. He and New Zealand's Mark Richardson dressing up in hooded one-piece running suits to do a hurdle race over kegs was one of those images that you won't forget (go on, Google it).

The Queensland boys still get a laugh about the aftermath of when the Bulls won the Sheffield Shield in 2011–12, beating Tasmania in a thriller at the Gabba. The celebrations were confined to the dressing-rooms well into the night, and at some point several of the players and Boof found themselves out on the ground. A mountain bike had appeared from somewhere, and with the ingenuity that comes from a long season, some liquid incentive and general tomfoolery, something like a ramp was cobbled together from plastic chairs and corflute signs.

Of course, dew and beer and water made for slippery conditions, but one of the daredevils successfully made it partially over the jump. That was enough for Boof. He ended up on the bike and, wobbling slightly, took a mighty go at hitting the ramp at speed. Physics, along with a lack of friction on a now very slippery sign, meant that Boof was like a roller coaster without the rails. He landed—hard. Eventually between groans and giggles, the thrillseekers abandoned their homemade stunt show and the night continued. By the next morning at recovery, Boof could hardly move. He had to go to the Indian Premier League for a coaching stint a day or two later, and by the time he had touched down in India, 'Crusty Demon' Lehmann was looking for the team doctor to treat his busted ribs and bruising.

My fortunes and fate have been tied to Darren for so long, that it stood to reason that when I faced the biggest decision of my career at the end of the 2007–08 season, he was one of the first people I went to for advice. Should I leave South Australia? As always, he was straight to the point. Where would I be happiest? Where would I play my best cricket?

The whole question of where I would be happiest was a double-edged one. Gavin and his family had moved from Sydney to Brisbane not long after Mum died and there was some symmetry about going there to be with him again. The other was a girl I had met recently.

Her name was Cherie, and we'd known each other in a circle of friends when we were teenagers. When she was eighteen she went out with one of the guys who played cricket and, Adelaide being the sort of place that it is, we'd see each other out and about.

One of Cherie's best friends, Amy, is the sister of one of my good mates, Damien, and so we were in similar circles over the years. I went to a wedding with Damien and other friends of ours and they were all into me—I was single and they all kept telling me to get in touch with Cherie.

And so, with a touch of Dutch courage, I did. We were friends on Facebook for a while and things were going nicely. It was just after Christmas when things got a bit more serious. Graham Manou was seeing the Australian runner Tamsyn Lewis and we had all got together to go to the Bay Sheffield, the famous Adelaide athletics meet. We enjoyed a big day and most of us ended up at a local tavern on the way home. Gav and his family were there and so at some point I was 'encouraged' to get Cherie to come and join us, and she did. She didn't quite realise the build-up I had given her. At some point I may have stated 'I'm going to introduce you to the girl I am going to marry ...' She managed to get through all of that in style, and so 27 December was when we started seeing each other.

I was torn with staying in Adelaide and seeing where things might go with the SACA, or making a fresh start with Queensland or WA (who were also keen). If I went to Queensland, I would be closer to Gav, and Dad had talked about potentially moving up as well.

A lot of people thought that I followed Boof to Queensland, but I was doing my talking to the then Queensland coach Terry Oliver, who handed over the Bulls coaching job to

Trevor Barsby by the time I moved there. There were a few portents though.

The last game of the season had been against Queensland and Jimmy Maher, the Bulls skipper, had announced he was retiring. Several of the senior campaigners in Australian cricket had jumped at the opportunity to join the new Indian Cricket League, which had been set up by a rival television network in India after they had been shut out of the equally new Indian Premier League. There had been a spate of retirements, as the new league was not sanctioned by the various governing bodies, and so intending players pretty well had to step down from their domestic teams.

As we enjoyed the last moments of the season in our dressing-room afterwards, Jimmy, who was a great mate of Boof's, sat beside me and popped his faded and beer-stiffened baggy maroon on my head.

'Looks good on you champ. You'll have your own inside twelve months I reckon,' he chirped.

I laughed it off, but obviously the lengthy and varied Maher/Lehmann conversations about cricket that had taken place over the summer had touched upon me at some stage and it had struck a chord with Jimmy.

Just how much of a chord became apparent when it came time to finalise my immediate future.

CHAPTER 12

LEAVING HOME

I never thought I'd leave South Australia. Playing cricket for the Redbacks was my dream as a kid and receiving that red cap was one of the proudest moments of my life—still is. But when it came time to negotiate a new contract towards the end of the 2007–08 season it quickly became clear that we had an issue.

I'd played on one-year contracts for my entire career, which I had no problem with as a younger guy who had probably suffered more than his fair share of injuries. I freely admit that my attitude and application in younger years left a lot to be desired on occasion, so I understood that the people in charge at the SACA wanted to play it safe with me. But having done a lot of growing up since Mum passed away and having put together my best season for South Australia, I felt like it was time that we made a longer-term commitment to each other.

In my early years with SA the fickle nature of professional sports wasn't something I really grasped, but I'd turned twenty-eight during that season and I knew that I was closer to the end of my career than the start.

I wanted the security of a three-year deal and that's where we hit a roadblock.

Rod Marsh, who was in charge of contracts at the SACA at the time, put a two-year deal on the table, but the contract made it clear that he wouldn't extend to a third year.

Rod was on my radar long before I was on his. Mum once sat on a plane alongside Rod when he was in charge of an Australian youth side that was going off on a tour. With a common interest in cricket, Mum managed to steer the conversation around to the fact that her schoolboy son was enjoying his cricket. Anyway, by the time the flight landed, Mum had in her possession a signed memento to inspire her young charge: 'To Ryan, all the best with your cricket, Rod Marsh.'

I have wondered occasionally whether I should have tabled that during my talks with the SACA when I was weighing up my future.

My management went back and forth with Rod, but nothing much really changed after their initial meetings. In the meantime, Queensland and Western Australia both made contact with my manager to put forward three-year deals.

The money was similar across all three offers, but SA wasn't willing to budge on the two-year contract that had been put on the table late in the season. I made it clear that I didn't want to leave, but also that I wouldn't be able to pass up the security of a three-year contract elsewhere.

It wasn't a bargaining position or a negotiating tool; I was going to take a three-year deal somewhere else if SA wasn't going to move. I had asked for a two-year deal at the end of the previous two seasons, but was offered one year each time. While I was disappointed with that, I was determined to go out and earn that multi-year deal, which I felt I had.

I finished that season with 37 Shield wickets, which put me in the top five wicket takers. As much as I loved playing for South Australia, the cold, hard truth of the matter was that I needed to make sure that my next contract was the very best one I could negotiate for myself and my family.

I felt like I was backing myself, but I didn't feel like the SACA offer reflected a great deal of confidence in me, which I think is really important. It was never about money and I was disappointed with a bit of press that suggested otherwise at the time.

I went over to Perth to meet Tom Moody, who was the Western Australia coach at the time, and I was really impressed with what he had to say. The Warriors had some real talent and had perhaps underachieved a little, so the prospect of joining them was certainly attractive, but Queensland had the edge if we couldn't work a deal with SA.

I'd played against the Bulls for years and I'd always admired how close they were as a team. It didn't seem to matter how well they were going or how much talent they had in their sides, the Queenslanders always showed a lot of passion and had plenty of team pride.

They'd been quite successful over the years, too, and the opportunity to play regular finals and win the Sheffield Shield was something I really craved. With Gav and his family living in Brisbane at the time as well, it just seemed like everything was falling into place.

As the negotiating process dragged on I started to feel that a change of environment might do me good. It didn't make it any easier to leave, but I think I needed to move out of my comfort zone and really test myself if I was going to take my cricket to the next level.

The decision was almost made for me, in a way, because they knew I was going to leave for a three-year deal and it was almost like they held the door open for me. They didn't do much—if anything—to hang on to me.

As it turned out I was in England when I made the decision to sign with Queensland for three years. I felt like I'd reached a crossroads in my career and a new challenge was the best direction for me to take.

I agonised over the decision, though. Although Gav was up in Queensland, I wasn't sure I could leave Dad, but he really encouraged me to do what was best for my cricket. Signing with Queensland ahead of Western Australia, meant that he wouldn't have to travel to either side of the country to visit us, which made me feel a bit better.

Telling guys like Mark Sorrell and Graham Manou, who I'd grown up playing cricket with, that I'd decided to leave was one of the hardest parts. Graham understood where I was coming from and Mark did too. It was difficult for him, though, because I think he was keen for me to stay, but he had no say in player contracts, so his hands were tied.

I was disappointed that the SACA chose not to match the three years that was on offer elsewhere, but I always had the greatest respect for Rod Marsh and I accepted that he had a plan for managing South Australia's squad. I certainly wasn't angry or bitter and I was determined to leave on good terms.

But I learned a harsh lesson after I did an interview in England shortly after I made the decision to leave. I felt the article that the journalist wrote from our chat didn't reflect what I was trying to say. I didn't want to be negative about the SACA—despite my disappointment—but that's how it came across.

The decision also brought an end to my brief stay with Sussex, who had signed me on the back of my British passport. My intention to play domestic cricket in Australia for three years meant I would be re-classified as an international player instead of a local, and they already had Mushtaq Ahmed in that spot.

When I got home I actually went to see Mike Deare, who was the chief executive of the SACA at the time, to set the record straight. I told him I had no ill feelings and apologised for what had been written. I loved being a Redback, but the time had come for both parties to move in different directions.

I believe I still would have played for Australia if I had stayed in South Austrlia but can't deny that a change of scenery, and pitch, certainly helped bring out the best in me. I think there was always a level of familiarity and comfort for me in playing for South Australia, despite the best efforts of guys such as Wayne Phillips.

I'd changed a lot, both as a person and as a cricketer, since I'd started with South Australia and I was ready for a new challenge.

Leaving my home and my close mates was tough, but it turned to excitement for me pretty quickly. I knew I'd made the right decision very early on. The Bulls had always seemed such a tight group to me and I wasn't sure how they'd take to an outsider, but I came into a very welcoming environment.

Chris Simpson was the skipper in my first season and he helped me feel at home. All of the guys were welcoming. There was a fair bit of golf and catching up for coffee early on, which helped a lot.

One of my few regrets about the decision to go to Queensland was that I didn't get to bowl with Mitch Johnson; he left for Western Australia during the same off-season.

The 2007–08 Shield season hadn't been a good one for the Bulls but, after finishing last that year, we started well in my first season. My body was holding up well, I was taking wickets and, most importantly, the team was performing well and putting points on the board.

It was a real learning experience for me to have the Gabba as my home wicket. I had always enjoyed bowling on Adelaide Oval: the new ball would go through quite nicely, then it would get old reasonably fast but, even then, it would start to reverse—I love working with that.

To see the ball go through at a nice pace at the Gabba for most of the day is obviously nice, but in saying that you do have to bowl a bit fuller. Quality Queensland batsmen such as Jimmy Maher and Martin Love will tell you that the toughest thing about batting at the Gabba is getting through the first couple of sessions on the first day when the ball is seaming around.

A lot of teams make the mistake of bowling too short at the Gabba, which allows the top-order batsmen to let a lot of balls through to the keeper. Late in the first session, or early in the second, the pitch will generally harden up and become a beautiful wicket to bat on.

It is hard because you do have to bowl a fuller length and it took me a little while to catch on to that fact. Once I did, adjusting my length really helped me to improve as a bowler.

Joe Dawes, who is a very good bowling coach, helped me a lot when I first moved up. He really helped me understand what I needed to do to bowl successfully at the Gabba (which helped me at other grounds too).

I felt like I was bowling reasonably well with Queensland and I wanted to make it into the Australian side, of course, but I wasn't hanging by the phone all day waiting for the call. I tried to focus on doing well for the Bulls and take whatever came from that.

I was at a barbecue at Gav's place in early January 2009 when I got a phone call to let me know I'd been picked for the Twenty20 squad to play against South Africa, who were coming off a 2–1 Test series win against Australia. We were set to play two T20 games against them, one in Melbourne and one in Brisbane, before a five-game one-day series.

Despite some decent form with the Bulls, selection in the Australian squad came out of the blue. Needless to say, I was pretty pumped!

I'd received plenty of cricket kit before, but I have to admit being issued with all my Australian team gear was a real buzz for me.

I carried the drinks in the first game. I would have loved to have played, but really I was just happy to be part of the squad for the first time. I took the opportunity to get to know the guys a bit better, some of whom I'd never met before. Davey Warner made a memorable debut. He made 89 off 43 balls, with seven 4s and six 6s, as he really got hold of the South African bowlers.

I had my fingers crossed for a call-up into the eleven for the second game at the Gabba, but it wasn't to be. I was twelfth man again and was largely a spectator as the boys took the series 2–0.

It was good to be a small part of a series win, but I was disappointed not to get a run in either of those games. I fully expected to rejoin Queensland after that, but Andrew Hilditch had some big news for me after that second T20 win; I'd been included in the squad for the one-day series as well: 'Go home and pack a bag!'

It was all a bit of a blur because I hadn't expected to be travelling and the squad was flying out the next day for the first one-dayer back at the MCG. It was all very exciting, but I carried the drinks again in a tight loss.

The next game was down in Hobart and I was hopeful of squeezing into the eleven. Shaun Tait had been carrying a niggle, but was set to play. When he felt it get a bit tight in the warm-up the decision was quickly made to pull him out. The next thing I knew I was in.

It had been a long time coming, but at twenty-nine years of age I was going to make my ODI debut for Australia.

In no time flat I went from carrying the drinks, to getting the nod to replace Taity, to having my cap presented by Ricky out on the ground.

My family wasn't in Hobart because I wasn't supposed to play, which was a shame, but I'll never forget standing there with the boys and shaking Ricky's hand as he presented me with my cap. It's a moment I'd wanted for so long—when it finally arrived it almost didn't seem real.

I couldn't tell you exactly what Ricky said because I was so in awe of the situation, but it was, basically, along the lines of 'Welcome to the club, you've worked hard to be here, you deserve it so enjoy it, but never take it for granted'.

I was the 169th player to represent Australia in an ODI. To be part of that select group is something I'll always cherish. It was great to be able to share that day with Davey Warner, who received his cap after me to become player 170.

Another important number was on my back: I'd chosen No 45 because Mum was born in 1945. It meant a lot to me to be able to honour her memory every time I went out on the field.

My head was spinning a bit, so I didn't mind at all when the skipper won the toss and chose to have a bat. It gave me a bit of time to sit back in the change rooms and get a feel for the game and what the pitch was doing.

It was a nice day in Hobart, which isn't often the case down there. I'd made my first-class debut for South Australia at Bellerive about eight years earlier and it seemed somehow fitting that I finally took the next step at the same ground.

I'd played in front of some decent-sized crowds before and even though it's not a large stadium by any means, it was a real buzz to play in front of over 15,000 people. Its size makes it feel like the fans are right on top of you, which is great.

I'd never enjoyed much success individually on that wicket, though. I generally found it to be quite flat and I never felt like I'd really got my head around how to bowl well on it.

I was keen to have a look at how two out-and-out champions approached the pitch. I'd always been a big fan of both Dale Steyn and Jacques Kallis, so I was really tuned in to how they were attacking the wicket in the conditions. I was keen to learn as much as I could before I had the ball in my hand.

The boys started out pretty well, but we fell in a bit of a hole, which meant that I went in to bat at No 9 with about three overs left. Like most bowlers, I always fancied myself as a batsman. If I'm honest, though, I've always found going in to bat more nerve-racking than any situation I've ever found myself in with the ball in hand.

We needed boundaries; but at least I managed to dab a few singles and get Brad Haddin on strike. I left our keeper high and dry late in the innings, though, when he drove the second-to-last ball into the non-striker's stumps and I set off running. Hadds had no chance and Makhaya Ntini ran him out easily.

I swung the bat at the last ball, but didn't get it nearly well enough and scooped it out to JP Duminy at deep mid-off on 7.

We made 249, which was probably a bit light on given how the wicket was playing. Shaun Marsh topped scoring with 78. Nathan Bracken and Ben Hilfenhaus opened the bowling and did really well to restrict them to 22 runs with the loss of 1 wicket after 9 overs. Then I came on for my first spell.

I've never been one to suffer from nerves too much, but I must admit it was a bit of a relief to hit a decent length with my first ball to Herschelle Gibbs, which he pushed out into the covers for no run.

My first over went for 5, which wasn't a bad start. Kallis got hold of me a bit in the second, which went for 9 runs. My figures weren't looking great when my third over went for 8: I had the job in front of me at 0–31 after 5 overs.

The South Africans had let the required run rate get away from them a bit when I came back on to bowl after 26 overs, but at 2–101 they had wickets in hand. I only bowled a couple of overs in that spell, which went for 5 runs, and I felt better about that.

Kallis was the danger man, but Hilf got the breakthrough when he dismissed him for 72 with David Hussey taking the catch at backward point. I came back on soon after, but got taken for another 9 runs as they looked to push the run rate up.

I was involved in a run-out after AB de Villiers slipped over coming back for a second run. I've always enjoyed fielding and it felt great to get involved. I always had it drummed into me that as a cricketer you're going to spend a lot of time in the field, so you may as well try to be the best you can at it and enjoy it. When I was younger I was reasonably quick and able to cover the ground quite well, which is always a big plus.

I used to love watching Ricky, Andrew Symonds, Mike Hussey and guys like that in the field. I put in a lot of time at training into fielding and catching. I always used to field at backward point or in the covers from early on in my Redbacks career and I used to love being so close to the action.

I came on to bowl my last 2 overs with South Africa 4–172 after 41 overs with the required run rate creeping towards 9 an over. I was desperate to contribute with a wicket and I was excited and relieved when Neil McKenzie played the first ball of my ninth over back onto his stumps. I can think of a few better ways to claim a wicket, but I didn't care how it had happened when all my teammates crowded around me to celebrate my maiden ODI scalp.

It came down to them needing 17 runs off the last over. They only managed 11 and the boys were really pleased to square the series at one win apiece. It was a reasonably subdued celebration, but having a few beers in the change rooms with the team was great.

I was happy with my own figures of 1–54 from 10 overs, but certainly not over the moon. I'd set myself to go for less than 6 runs an over as an absolute minimum goal, which I was able to do, and my pace was up around the mid-140s, which is usually a sign that I'm in a decent rhythm.

There's generally not much time to celebrate, with the Australian fixture being quite crowded, but it was nice to be able to have a bit of time with the boys to have a chat about the day. It had been a big experience for me and a massive learning curve, but that would be it for my summer in the Aussie set-up. Taity came back in for the third ODI and I went back to play for Queensland, which wasn't unexpected.

I was happy just to get a taste of playing for Australia and learn from the experience. Unfortunately, I wasn't able to break back into the side for over a year. It had been a big summer for me, but I was about to encounter a series of setbacks that threatened to derail my international career before it had even started.

CHAPTER 13

SWINGS AND ROUNDABOUTS

I was playing in my second Shield game for Queensland after my brief stint with the Australian squad when I broke my foot.

It was my first game back at the Adelaide Oval since leaving the Redbacks. It was a big deal for me to go back to the ground I'd played so much cricket on as a Bulls player and to see all of my former teammates again. But it turned out to be a tough match for me and the team.

Victoria was the standout side that season, but we were right in the hunt to join the Bushrangers in the Shield final with three rounds to play. It went bad for me early, though. Daniel Harris smashed the ball back at me in the first innings and I stuck my right foot out to stop it. I connected so well that it bounced out to the fielder at mid-wicket. It hurt a fair bit at the time, but I didn't think anything was too wrong because I bowled another 5 overs or so in that spell.

But as I cooled down a bit in the field it really started to throb. I hobbled off to get a new pair of boots and went back on. When I tried to chase a ball at one point I just fell over because the pain was so excruciating when I pushed off on the foot.

They sent me in for an X-ray the same day, but even then I didn't think anything was seriously wrong. It came as a real shock to me when the doc told me I'd broken a bone and done a pretty decent job of it too.

I didn't bat in our first dig and we declared 189 runs behind the Redbacks, who came out looking for quick runs in their second innings to extend their lead. Chris Swan bowled really well, taking 3 wickets, but we had the job ahead of us chasing a target of 333 for the outright win.

The coach wasn't going to let me bat. At tea it looked like we were at least going to hang on for the draw, or even take the win, after a strong performance from the middle order. It was going to go down to the wire, so I hobbled out and did what I could. I made 11 runs before I was the last man out, caught by Cullen Bailey off the bowling of Mark Cleary, with the team still 20 runs behind. To have put ourselves in a position to win it, or at least draw, after a rocky start was an amazing effort by the boys—it was a bloody tough loss to take.

My anger and frustration were compounded by the fact that I needed an operation to insert a plate on my fifth metatarsal (the bone on the outer edge of my foot). It was a bad break, which would keep me sidelined for at least a month.

That frustration only grew as the Bulls made the one-day final, which they won against the Vics at the MCG, and then set up a Sheffield Shield final, also against the Bushrangers.

I was absolutely delighted for the boys because they'd worked their backsides off to be in that position—but I'm never more unhappy than when I can't contribute.

The Shield final took place just under a month after I'd had my foot operated on. I tried to get up for it, but the medical advice was that the risk of doing more damage and spending longer on the sidelines was too great.

Sitting there and watching the boys draw that match, which handed the Sheffield Shield win to Victoria, was one of the more unpleasant experiences of my career to that point.

I was cleared to go and join the Indian Premier League side Deccan Chargers for the start of the League's second season in April. I was still getting some soreness in my foot when I bowled in the nets early on and I was starting to be a bit concerned that there might be something more to the injury. But then the pain just went away.

I got up one morning and decided I wasn't going to be tentative on it; I was going to go out into the nets, let rip and see what happened. To my great relief I bowled pain-free for the first time in about three months and was able to enjoy a good series with Deccan.

* * *

I signed a short-term contract with Surrey in June that year. I was looking to re-establish myself in the longer game and get as much bowling under my belt as I could ahead of the Australian summer.

I felt a bit rusty, but picked up a couple of wickets in a drawn four-day match against Glamorgan in Cardiff before we headed to Northampton to take on Northamptonshire. I loved being back in the thick of an English domestic season and was keen to take my game up a notch. Instead I suffered an injury that threatened to bring an abrupt end to my career.

The Surrey skipper, former England batsman Mark Butcher, won the toss and sent Northamptonshire in to bat and we were ripping through them at a decent rate.

I'd taken a wicket and was feeling good when I pulled up in my seventeenth over. As I ran into the wicket I heard a sharp crack and experienced a shooting pain through my right knee. It felt like it had locked up. I tried to work it loose and bowl another couple of balls, but the skipper told me to get off the ground and get it looked at.

The Surrey physios worked on me for a bit but, as it happened, the Australian team was camped up in Leicester, about an hour up the M1. I arranged to go and meet up with team physio Alex Kountouris. The Aussie team had been eliminated from the ICC World Twenty20 tournament just days before and the focus had switched to preparing for the upcoming Ashes series.

Alex assessed me and didn't like what he saw; but he needed a specialist's opinion. Mr David Young, a renowned surgeon based in Melbourne who did a lot of work for

Cricket Australia, was actually in the south of England for a conference at the time so Alex set up a meeting. I wouldn't be bowling again for Surrey in that match, but I batted with a runner and actually made my highest first-class innings: 94! We won the match comfortably, then I was quickly onto a train and off to see David.

I took some scans with me and David determined that I had damaged the lateral meniscus (basically, the material that cushions the joint). There was also a degenerative cyst that would need arthroscopic surgery to repair. The recovery time wouldn't be extensive but, as I was only on a short-term contract with Surrey, my time in England was over.

I was still quite new to the Australian set-up then and it was decided that, as Queensland Cricket would be footing my medical bills, I would have the surgery done by a Brisbane surgeon. He was a highly respected practitioner, so I had no problem with that. But two months after the initial surgery things still weren't right with my knee. I couldn't bowl without sharp pain and I was suffering a lot of swelling.

I was operated on again in September, but the results were basically the same—more pain and more swelling.

I'd already missed the start of the Sheffield Shield season when I went back in for a consult with the surgeon. I was desperate to get the problem sorted because if I was going to push my claims for a re-call to the Australian side, in any form of cricket, then I needed to be performing with the Bulls.

I was absolutely blindsided when the surgeon told me that perhaps I had better start thinking about life after cricket. I sat there speechless and listened as he explained what was wrong with my knee; why what he'd done hadn't fixed it; and why he felt my prognosis wasn't good.

Dad had come with me and as soon as we left the surgeon's office I said to him straight out that retirement wasn't even on the cards. Still, I was stunned by what I'd just heard and more than a little worried that he might be correct in his assessment of my knee.

I felt like my international career was slipping through my fingers before it had even really begun. All I wanted was an opportunity to put my best foot forward. If I wasn't good enough to play at the top level then I could live with that; but I couldn't cop getting tripped up by a bung knee.

I rang Alex and he was great. I was pretty fired up, but he calmed me down and told me to get on a plane to Melbourne and see Mr Young. I was on edge going in to see him.

I took all my scans and medical files from the past few months. Luckily, he saw things a bit differently. I fully expected to have to go under the knife again, but he suggested a less invasive approach with a far quicker recovery period, which was music to my ears.

The cyst in my knee was responsible for a fair amount of the inflammation and pain, so David 'aspirated' it—which basically means he stuck a big needle into it and drew some fluid out. There was a bit more to it than that—and I'm not sure what he did differently from my initial surgeon—but I was just happy that I'd been given a chance to play cricket that summer.

I saw David on 19 November and I played in a one-day match for the Bulls on 9 December, then followed it up in their last Shield game before the Christmas break at the Gabba two days later.

I didn't bowl well, mind you, but I bowled! I was a bit tentative in 6 overs in the one-dayer, but I sent down 40 overs in a 9-wicket win for Queensland and I was over the moon. Mr David Young was on speed dial on my phone from that point.

The Bulls went into Twenty20 mode after Christmas and, although I was still feeling my way with my knee a bit, I was slowly growing in confidence and took 8 wickets in the series before we got knocked out in the preliminary final by Victoria.

I worked with Alex and the Queensland boys to come up with a plan to keep up the fitness I needed because running put too much strain on my knee. I'd never been a great runner anyway, so I didn't mind this at all.

I needed strong legs to help keep me on the field and I took to riding a stationary bike twice a day, which was much better for me than pounding the pavement.

It was about being smart. It wasn't about getting as fit as I could, it was about doing whatever it took to make sure I could bowl. I needed bowling fitness if I was going to be of any use to a team and everything in my exercise program was tailored towards achieving that goal.

I would have ridden a unicycle while juggling flaming batons if they told me it was going to help keep me on the field. I felt like I'd dodged a bullet; my career was back on my own terms.

CHAPTER 14

ONE HOT SUMMER

I didn't allow myself to think about getting back into the Australian side as I came back from my knee troubles. I wasn't one of the twenty-five players to be given a Cricket Australia contract at the start of that season—I didn't expect I would be—but that was a fair indication of where I sat in the national selectors' calculations that summer. I just wanted to work back into some fitness and slowly regain some bowling rhythm with Toombul and Queensland.

I knew that if I started to take a few wickets for the Bulls then the rest would take care of itself. I wanted to enjoy being back in a team environment. I focussed in on the process of working back to peak fitness and if returning to the Australian team was one of the outcomes of that process then so be it. If it wasn't then I'd at least know I'd done everything I could.

I was sitting in a cafe around the corner from the Gabba in late January when I got the call to get on a flight to

Adelaide that afternoon. Australia was playing Pakistan in an ODI at Adelaide Oval and Peter Siddle was under an injury cloud. They wanted me there on standby in case he didn't get up.

The Aussies already held a 2–0 lead in the five-game series, which followed their 3–0 Test series whitewash of Pakistan, who were touring along with the West Indies in the Australian summer of 2009–10.

Australia had kicked off the series at the Gabba just days earlier, but I was playing grade cricket for Toombul that weekend. We'd won the Twenty20 grand final on the Sunday, so I was in pretty good spirits even before I got the phone call from Cricket Australia informing me that I had been called into the ODI squad.

It was just over a year since I'd made my ODI debut down in Hobart against South Africa and there had been plenty of times since when I thought that might be it for me on the international scene.

After my all-too-brief taste of international cricket, my mind and body had copped a hammering during a torturous twelve months that saw me sitting in doctors' surgeries more often than playing out in the middle.

All of that was the furthest thing from my mind, though, as I excitedly threw my kit into a bag and headed for the airport.

It was great to be back amongst the boys again after such a long break. Ricky was really welcoming and my excitement reached a new level when I was told that Sidds had a sore back and they were going to give him a rest. I was in.

I had made my ODI debut against South Africa, but the match against Pakistan over twelve months later was really where it all started for me as an international cricketer.

You only make one debut, but my appearance against the South Africans was more of a false start than the beginning of my international career. I didn't know it at the time, of course, but the match against Pakistan set in motion a series of events that saw my career gather some real momentum.

It will always be special to me that such a pivotal match in my career took place at Adelaide Oval in front of all my friends and family. I knew what a massive opportunity it was for me, but I was quite calm going into the game. It was a day/nighter, so I took it easy that morning and by the time we arrived at the ground I was focussed on doing everything I needed. But most of all, I was going to go out there and have fun.

Ricky won the toss and had a bat, which allowed the bowlers to have a bit of a look at what the pitch was doing. Dougie Bollinger, Clint McKay and Shane Watson were the other seamers, with Nathan Hauritz, in to try to get a bit of turn on the Adelaide wicket.

Shaun Marsh and Michael Clarke made 83 and 80 respectively in a total of 6–286, which was a decent score. As is generally the case in Adelaide, it was a very good pitch for batsmen, so we'd need to bowl well.

It was such a buzz to walk out onto Adelaide Oval, where I'd played so much cricket for the Redbacks, as a member of the Australian cricket team. I've always loved the ground and to be out there representing my country in front of so many people that were important to me was really special.

I had been hoping to open the bowling—I really wanted to try to get my eye in early—and Ricky granted my wish. I came on from the Cathedral end after Dougie had kicked off proceedings. I had a thought for Mum at the top of my mark and ran in to bowl to Kamran Akmal. He prodded it away for a single to mid-on. What few nerves I did have were gone because I was right in the moment after that.

I was happy with how they were coming out, but I was ecstatic when Akmal shuffled across his stumps 5 balls later and I hit him on the pads. We all went up and umpire Asoka de Silva gave him out LBW without hesitating. All the boys were great as they came in to celebrate; they were really encouraging and I couldn't help but think how good this was after some of the down moments I'd been through.

I bowled 5 overs in that opening spell and I was pleased to have only conceded 16 runs when I came off. The boys had Pakistan in trouble at 4–60, but Fawad Alam and Umar Akmal did well to steady the ship and advance the score to 4–144 by the time I came back on at the City end. I went for 7 in my first over back, but then I managed to coax an edge from Akmal that went straight to Brad Haddin for the breakthrough.

I bowled a couple of overs in that spell before coming back on at the Cathedral end. Shahid Afridi really had his eye in and was tipping the scales in his side's favour with a typically blistering knock of 36 off 27 balls. They needed 61 runs from 41 balls after my first ball of that spell disappeared to the boundary. I've always admired the way that Afridi handled a bat and he was particularly dangerous at Adelaide

Oval with its short square boundaries. He made a bit of space for himself as I came in to bowl my second ball and I fired in a yorker that got through him and hit the middle stump about 10 cm from the base. I'd tried and failed to bowl the same ball a few times. As a bowler there are few better feelings than when you get a fast, straight yorker right through a batsman on middle stump.

Umar Gul swung for the square-leg fence later that same over and only succeeded in sending the ball rocketing straight up into the air. They can be really tricky ones to catch, but Hadds made no mistake. My dream night was complete when Naved-ul-Hasan tried to smack the first delivery of my next over, but lobbed it to Cameron White at mid-wicket instead.

You couldn't write that script; I'd worked hard to give myself another chance, but to grasp that opportunity with a five-for and hold that ball up to the crowd was about the best feeling I'd had in cricket to that point. Actually, the best feeling I had that day was when I found Dad before we left the field and gave him a hug over the fence.

I was named Man of the Match by the Channel Nine team, which came with a cheque for $2500, but I was more satisfied at having come in and done my bit for the side. I was quickly reminded that all individual prize money goes into the team kitty!

We sang 'Under the Southern Cross I stand' to mark the series win—I'd never actually heard it all the way through before. We won my first game against South Africa in Hobart, but the victory song only comes out after a series win in one-day cricket. I was in the middle of the circle and I had the words written down on a little piece of paper, which was a bit embarrassing. But once I got the hang of it I threw the paper away and sang it loud and proud. It's such a passionate, proud Australian song. That was a moment that will stay with me forever.

I was going to travel with the team to Perth, which had been the plan before I played in Adelaide, so we didn't have much time to celebrate. If I had carried the drinks in Adelaide they were going to give me a game in Perth regardless, but I was happy that I'd earned my spot. Dad and Bill, Cherie's dad, and a few mates came back to my hotel room and we sat around and had a few quiet beers.

I preferred that to a huge celebration because we had a great time chatting about the day and it allowed Dad to tell me about his experience of it as well.

I was determined to build on the foundation I'd laid in Adelaide, but I never dreamed I could follow up that five-for with another one … conceding fewer runs to boot!

I finished with 5–19, but I had a lot of help. Cameron White took a brilliant catch, diving to his left after I got one to go away from Salman Butt in the first over of the Pakistan innings. Hadds did the business to send Younis Khan on his way and I had a bit of luck go my way when Umar Akmal tried to drop the ball at his feet for a quick single only to see it bounce back onto his off-stump and barely dislodge the bail.

Naved-ul-Hasan tickled one straight to Hadds next ball and I found myself on a hat-trick! The crowd was making all kinds of noise and my heart was racing as I went in to bowl at Iftikhar Anjum. I tried to trap him in front, but he got his bat down on it just in time.

Hadds did the right thing by me again when he took a brilliant one-handed catch going to his right to dismiss Iftikhar Anjum and hand us a 135-run win. It was a great moment to share with Hadds; he's a real heart and soul–type player. All of the boys were welcoming in those early days, but he really helped me understand what it meant to play cricket for Australia. His passion for cricket and representing his country is infectious and I have a lot to thank him for.

* * *

I've always enjoyed watching the West Indies play, so it was a great thrill to play against them for the first time. They'd been well beaten in the Test series against Australia before Christmas, but they were going to be a different proposition in the one-day format.

The five-game series kicked off directly after we beat Pakistan 5–0 and I was happy enough with how I bowled in the first match in Melbourne. I picked up 3 wickets for 24 runs in a 113-run win that got us off to just the start we were after.

I was rested for the next game in Adelaide, which was the last thing I felt like doing, but I understood the reasons behind it. We play so much cricket these days that the risk of burnout for bowlers is high, but no player likes to miss games. I certainly didn't fancy giving up my spot having waited so long to get into the Australian team!

The boys had another solid win, which meant we'd go to Sydney looking to clinch the series. The West Indies put in a good performance with the ball to keep us to 225 runs, but the match was eventually abandoned one over into their innings after heavy rain hit the SCG.

I hate rain depriving me of the opportunity to play cricket. Sitting in the dressing-rooms that night watching the rain bucket down was as frustrating as it always felt, no matter who I was playing for. It was interesting to see how the different guys dealt with it, though. We're not allowed to have any electronic communication devices, including iPads, in the rooms due to strict anti-corruption rules, so it makes it a bit tricky to try to pass the time. A few guys played cards and others read the paper. I was just happy to get around and have a bit of a chat with whoever was about.

We won the series up in Brisbane, but I didn't have the best time of it. Chris Gayle and Kieron Pollard really got hold of me at various stages, so I had to go to Plan B—and even C or D— to try to stem the flow of runs. I managed a couple of wickets, but conceded 64 runs, which is obviously way too much.

Ricky Ponting, Shane Watson and James Hopes all scored half-centuries in a very even performance by our batsmen to set the West Indies a target of 325 in the last game of the series at the MCG. We were determined to go through the summer undefeated and we managed that convincingly with a similar effort from the bowlers with all five of us taking at least one wicket to dismiss the West Indians for 199.

I didn't want that Australian summer to end. Like batsmen who peel off a few big scores in a row, bowlers can find themselves 'in the zone'. I felt like I'd never bowled better. It might sound a bit odd, but bowling in those series against Pakistan and the West Indies almost felt effortless at times.

I was bowling fast, finding a good length and swinging the ball. I felt like I was putting the ball where I wanted it and doing exactly what I wanted with it. That was quite a rare feeling in my experience, so it's one of those things that you've really got to enjoy while it's happening. Cricket's a bloody tough game to play and there'll be plenty of other times when it's not going your way.

I've gone through times when I don't feel like I'm bowling that well and the wickets still come, but there are other times I feel like I'm really hitting the mark, but I can't get a wicket to save myself. It's funny how it works sometimes, but everything seemed to be working for me that summer.

When I was younger I really struggled with consistency. I guess I realised at some point that to be successful I needed to work hard to achieve the consistency I needed in my game. I did a lot more target bowling in the nets; it wasn't rocket science, it was just about sheer repetition.

Instead of bowling 6 overs in practice and trying several different types of deliveries, I would pick one—an outswinger for example—and I'd just try to hit that thirty-six times. I'd do the same the next day with my bouncer and so on. It's all about getting the ball in the right spot and building that confidence to know that you can do it no matter what the situation.

I love bowling for my country—it's exciting and gets me quite pumped up. At the same time, I've always found that one of the keys to bowling well is being able to control the adrenaline rush that comes with it.

Whenever I do school clinics I always get kids asking me how they can bowl really fast. My answer is: the harder you try to bowl fast, the slower it will come out. Many times in my career I've tried to steam in as fast as I could and bowl as fast as I could and the ball has actually come out all wrong and been slower as a result. It's a fine line.

It's all about getting your action right, being comfortable in your approach to the wicket and establishing a good 'feel' at the crease, so that you're not thinking too much about the mechanics of your action.

If I come in and I'm feeling really balanced and I'm timing things well, that's when I tend to bowl my best. If I feel rushed, then things will get out of whack. If I feel like I'm getting off my back foot too quickly in my action, if I'm pushing too hard, basically, then I'm out of rhythm.

There's a lot going on when you try to explain it to someone, but my bowling action has always seemed quite natural to me. I get asked what changed in my bowling action for me to achieve some success late in my career, but I feel like my action has been basically the same all the way through.

I got a little bit heavier as I approached my thirties, which may have helped with my momentum as I approach the crease, and I probably started running in a little bit quicker, but there was never any radical alteration to my action that saw me break through to the next level.

I need to hit the crease with momentum, but without trying to come in too fast. If you talked to half a dozen quick bowlers about their actions, most would give you a similar idea of what they're trying to do at the crease—but you might also get six different descriptions of what they look for in terms of establishing their own feel or rhythm. Although we're all trying to achieve the same thing, different things work for different bowlers and—after you've got a firm grasp on the basics—it's just a matter of finding what works for you.

For me, it's mainly about knowing which ball I'm going to bowl and visualising the point on the pitch that I'm going to hit. I try to keep it pretty simple. A lot of the time, for me, the batsman isn't even part of that process.

I've got certain marks that I need to hit where I'll gain pace in my run-up, but mainly I'll just get my grip for the ball I want to bowl and focus on hitting the keeper at a certain point. Whether it's his gloves or his hat or even further than that … maybe a point in the crowd behind him.

But most of the time it's about putting the ball in a certain spot and, if it's good enough, it will get most batsmen out regardless of who it is.

* * *

I remember someone asking me what it felt like to be an Australian ODI cricketer soon after I made my debut in January 2009. I replied that I wouldn't think of myself in those terms until I'd played ten games at a minimum. I don't know why ten was significant to me, but I thought that if I played one or two international matches and then just drifted out of the picture then all that effort would still really be for nothing.

If I played ten games then I would consider myself an Aussie one-day cricketer because at least I would have been able to stick around for a little while. I didn't know it then, but it appeared more likely than not that my international career would be a flash in the pan as the events of 2009 unfolded.

So it was with a great deal of satisfaction that I played my tenth ODI for Australia in March 2010, which happened to be against New Zealand at Eden Park in Auckland.

My big summer had reached another high point for me when I was told that I'd been selected to go on my first international tour with the Australian team. I was absolutely thrilled to head over to New Zealand with the boys because I thought it would be an excellent opportunity to keep growing as a cricketer and also cement some of the relationships that I'd established over that summer.

I'd never been to New Zealand before, so I was keen to test myself in different conditions. I'd always enjoyed going on tour when I was with a few development squads earlier in my career. There's something about being away from home with all your mates, playing on enemy turf in front of hostile crowds—it brings teammates together.

I wasn't happy with the way I bowled in the first game of the series: I finished with 1–57 in a 2-wicket loss, and I was determined to bounce back. We batted first and set them a decent target of 273, but they'd chased down 275 in the first game, so we had to bowl well.

I'd only conceded 7 runs from my first 3 overs when I trapped Peter Ingram in front with the fourth ball of my fourth over. Neil Broom came in and I caught him on the crease for another huge LBW shout. Umpire Rudi Koertzen sent him on his way and suddenly I was on a hat-trick. James Franklin was facing, but I didn't make him play the ball, which is the last thing you want to do as a bowler in that situation.

I was still happy to have chipped in with a couple of wickets, though, because the Kiwis had gotten off to a decent start. We went off for a rain interruption, which changed the equation for New Zealand thanks to the Duckworth–Lewis system. They were making good progress before Mitch Johnson slowed their run rate with a couple of important wickets.

They needed 14 runs off 12 balls when I came on to bowl my last over, but they were down to their last partnership with Daniel Vettori and Tim Southee at the crease. Vettori was the danger man with 70 runs, but he tried to make some room for himself and I hit off-stump. It was a great feeling to have done my bit after an off performance. It was also a little bit special for me, having reached my own personal ten-game milestone in decent style.

I played in the next two games, in Hamilton and Auckland, and was reasonably happy with my form before I was given a rest for the last ODI of the series. We won both of those games to give ourselves an unbeatable 3–1 lead and I was stoked to be part of Australia's third ODI series win in a row.

I have a permanent reminder of that series, and my tenth match in particular, because I got a tattoo of the Southern Cross with my one-day number (169) on the inside of my left forearm. It was a massive summer for me—more than I could have asked or hoped for.

Since I'd received that surprise call-up to the Australian ODI squad against Pakistan in Adelaide on 26 January, Australia Day 2010, I'd played a total of eleven ODIs against three teams across two countries in just 45 days. The significance of that period wasn't lost on me. I still have fond memories of it years later.

CHAPTER 15

MY BAGGY GREEN

I never thought I'd play Test cricket.

For me, making the Australian one-day side was a realistic goal and when T20 cricket started to emerge I thought making either of those two teams was something I could aim for.

But everything changed during that Australian summer of 2009–10. So much went right for me. I was riding a wave of momentum; I felt like I was in the best form of my life and I'd never enjoyed playing cricket more. Perhaps, most importantly though, I felt like we were finding ways to manage my knee.

As that summer progressed I started to hear a bit of talk about a possible Test debut for me down the track and that's really when I started to think it might be possible. It wasn't going to be easy because the Test team was in excellent form with series wins against Pakistan and the West Indies that same summer. Mitch Johnson, Peter Siddle, Dougie Bollinger, Shane Watson and Ben Hilfenhaus were all getting the job done with the ball, so I was still a fair way down the pecking order.

With a strong Aussie summer under my belt and some decent form in the one-dayers against the Kiwis in New Zealand I was confident in my ability to play Test cricket if given the chance. Still, it came as a huge surprise to me when I was told I had been picked in the side to play the first Test against New Zealand in Wellington.

It was an odd feeling; I knew I'd put myself in a good position to get picked, but I hadn't dared allow myself to think that it could happen. When it did happen I was absolutely blown away.

I knew I was bowling well and I was going on a Test tour, but I just wanted to get over there and really have a crack at the one-day series. I certainly didn't have any expectations of breaking into the Test side—given my age and injury history.

But suddenly there it was right in front of me: the baggy green cap that so many Aussie kids dream of. While my one-day debut for Australia happened so fast that none of my family were there to watch, I got the life-changing news that I would play my first Test match for my country enough in advance that some important people could share the experience with me. Dad, Gav and Cherie were as excited as I was—Dad probably even more so—when I told them I'd been picked and they all hopped on a plane to come over and share what was going to be a huge moment in my life.

Surprise, surprise, I was actually under a bit of an injury cloud going into that Test. I'd carried a side strain through the last couple of matches in the one-day series and actually missed a game because of it.

The selectors must have been reasonably concerned over my ability to come up for the Test because they flew South Aussie quick Peter George over as cover. But I knew my body pretty well by then and I was confident I'd be fit. I'd had a few side strains over the journey, I knew what it felt like to have a bad one, and this wasn't going to be enough to stop me making my Test debut. That baggy green was right there in front of me and there was absolutely no way I was going to allow anyone else to jump in front of me!

I wouldn't have put my hand up if I thought I was in any danger of breaking down, but I bowled a few overs without too much discomfort, then pulled up pretty well.

I actually slept really well the night before the first Test. Even though I was hugely excited to be making my Test debut I think the fact that I was older and had been around the one-day side helped me relax a bit. But that all changed when I woke up the morning of the match and the nerves kicked in. Still, it was an amazing feeling heading to the ground knowing I was about to represent my country in a Test match.

Dad, Gav and Cherie had arrived in Wellington in plenty of time, but they didn't see me receive my baggy green.

I told them all to get to the ground nice and early so they could get a good spot. They did their part and were there well ahead of time, but the security guards at the gate wouldn't let them in! They tried to explain the situation, but the guards weren't having it.

They went around to the administration building and told their story and an official overheard them talking and told them to follow him inside. They were taken up a bunch of stairs and came out in a dining room where Dad reckons he saw the team break up after the presentation and walk off the ground. It was disappointing they got so close and couldn't be there for such a huge moment in my life, but I appreciated the effort!

Ricky Ponting presented me with my baggy green. I'd idolised Punter growing up and it's hard to describe just what it meant to me to be standing there and receiving that famous cap from him.

I used to see guys getting their baggy greens on the field before a Test on the television and think how good a feeling that must be. I always imagined it would be amazing, and it was, but it was also quite a surreal experience too. It had been a huge deal for me to receive my first red South Australian cap and then my maroon Queensland cap—I cherished and loved those caps and guarded them with my life—but to be handed a baggy green was another step up.

Ricky said a few kind words and told me that what I was about to receive was the ultimate goal of every person playing cricket in Australia. He told me that I was part of an exclusive club now and explained how important it was that I look after my baggy green.

I was really humbled to hear those words. He was really encouraging as well. He said that I was in that position for a reason and that I shouldn't change what I'd been doing to get myself there. He wanted me to enjoy the moment and my first Test, which he hoped was the first of many to come.

Anyone who is privileged enough to earn a baggy green will tell you what an honour it is, but at my age, with so many years of cricket behind me, it really floored me.

I'd worked hard for a long time—I'd tripped over my own feet plenty of times along the way—and I'd finally earned the right to play alongside the best players in the country. It was a dream come true and a moment I'll always cherish.

Punter won the toss and chose to bat, which wasn't a bad thing as far as I was concerned because it allowed me to sit back and get a bit of a feel for the game. It also allowed me to take in my first experience of a Test dressing-room. I'd played enough first-class cricket to be able to keep the nerves under control, but there's no doubt I was really excited. Despite having a fair bit of experience, I didn't know a lot of the guys in the side at the time all that well, so I was keen to get to know them a bit as blokes as well as cricketers.

I hit it off with Mitch Johnson right off the bat and we've been good mates ever since. I'd played in a few junior squads with Nathan Hauritz and Dougie Bollinger, and knew a few of the guys a bit from the one-day side. But I was pretty keen to really establish stronger relationships with all the boys.

The top order put on a solid start, but it was the partnership between Michael Clarke and Marcus North that really set us up. Pup came in when we were 3–115 and was still there at stumps on day one with a century to his name. He went on to score 168 in one of the great batting performances I've seen, with North making a ton of his own before Punter declared at 5–459.

Michael had been going through a highly publicised relationship break-up with Lara Bingle at the time and had flown back to Australia the week of the Test. It was a big decision for him to fly home given the level of media scrutiny he was under, but the character and mental toughness he showed during what was a really difficult time was amazing.

To have something so personal play out in the media would test the best of us, but his ability to show absolute focus on the task at hand was unbelievable. I was still getting to know Michael at that stage, but I really respected the way he handled himself during that period. I've never had to deal with that sort of media focus and, for me, the way he was able to come through it and perform said a lot about the character of the man.

I really like to watch as many balls as I can when we're batting and that's probably been the case for as far back as I can remember. Obviously, I like to see how my teammates are going, but I always found it really helpful to watch and get a feel for what opposition bowlers are doing and how the wicket's playing.

I hadn't actually played on Basin Reserve before I made my Test debut there. I'd had a brief bowl out in the middle, but with the conditions being a bit damp we could only bowl off a short run, which wasn't an ideal preparation.

I spent a fair part of our first innings thinking about how I was going to bowl into the wind if I had to because it was pretty ferocious. They don't call it 'Windy Wellington' for nothing; I even saw a heavy roller get pushed onto the ground, the wind was that fierce! Dealing with the conditions wouldn't be easy for any of us, but when the time came I was mostly able to shut out those concerns and focus in on the basics. I just wanted to land the first ball somewhere near the mark and get through the first over, then try to build some momentum.

The Test team had obviously had a really good summer— it really struck me how much their performance with the bat reminded me of the golden era under Steve Waugh. The batsmen had done their part and posted a big score and now the bowlers had to do their bit and pile on the pressure with the ball.

My baggy green had barely left my head since I had received it and I decided it would be my hat of choice in the field. It's a bit of an unwritten rule that everyone wears it for the first hour or so of the first session anyway, but I decided that for as long as I played Test cricket I'd wear that beautiful green cap whenever I fielded.

The Australian summer has got the better of me a few times since and I've donned the wide-brimmed floppy hat to keep the sun off, but it could have been 50°C that first day in Wellington and I still would have worn my baggy green. Fortunately, it was actually quite cool that day.

I wasn't expecting to open the bowling with Doug Bollinger and Mitch Johnson bowling as well as they were, but Ricky threw me the new ball. I would be running straight into the teeth of what felt like a full-strength cyclone.

Dougie had opened at the other end and trapped BJ Watling in front with his fifth ball, so we were up and about. My goal was to keep the pressure on and bowl a maiden.

Tim McIntosh was on strike and I managed to get my first ball in Test cricket through to Brad Haddin behind the stumps, which was a bit of a relief. My next ball was a wide, but that was the only score I conceded so I was pretty happy with that.

I felt like I bowled reasonably well those first few overs and my figures weren't too bad without getting a wicket. I wasn't too tense—generally I'm more nervous going in to bat than going in to bowl—and I had found a reasonable rhythm.

Ricky gave me a lot of confidence; if something wasn't working he'd have a chat and give me some advice or we'd try something a bit different. I always found him very easy to communicate with; he was always approachable and happy to hear what I had to say.

I was obviously pretty keen to break through for my first Test wicket, but I had Ricky and a few of the more senior guys in my ear telling me to just concentrate on sticking to our plan for each batsman and not try to force something to happen. You can tend to 'over-attack' when you're desperate for a wicket and that's generally when things can go pear-shaped.

I just wanted to put the ball in the right spots and push it through to the keeper. I bowled 5 overs in my first spell, which included a couple of maidens, but I couldn't make the breakthrough I wanted.

Thankfully I didn't have to wait too long, though. McIntosh had faced 57 balls for his 9 runs when he attempted to drive the fourth ball of my seventh over of the day and edged it to gully where Mike Hussey took a sharp catch. It was all a bit of a blur as the boys came from all over the ground to shake my hand and slap me on the back, but I certainly remember it being a massive relief to have a wicket on the board.

Dougie struck again to have the Kiwis in trouble at 4–44, but Martin Guptill and Daniel Vettori managed to put on a decent partnership that saw them bat through until stumps. We were keen to break that partnership early on the third day and I was really happy when I managed to coax an edge from Vettori in the first over of the day with Punter taking a sharp catch at second slip. I didn't manage another wicket, but Dougie and Mitch ripped through the line-up to have them all out for 157.

There was a fair bit of discussion over whether Punter would enforce the follow-on because they hadn't worked out as well as he'd liked a few times in the past. We hadn't bowled that many overs and the conditions were quite cool, so the bowlers were happy to have another crack. I think we all wanted to try to press home the advantage and get the win in the bag. Ricky asked me how I was feeling, but I'd barely felt the side strain that bothered me before the match, so I was ready to go.

We hoped that if we bowled well enough we might be able to finish the game that day, but they batted a lot better. After a confidence-boosting start, I was really happy with the way I was able to bowl in the second innings and finished with figures of 4–77. As pleased as I was, I was kicking myself at one point when I dropped Daryl Tuffey off my own bowling to miss out on what would have been a very memorable five-for.

New Zealand did well to make us bat again on the last day, but Phil Hughes and Simon Katich opened and made the 106 runs necessary before lunch. It was an amazing feeling and something I'll never forget. I'd sung 'Under the Southern Cross I stand' with the boys after one-day series wins against Pakistan and the West Indies, but it seemed even more special as part of the Test team to belt out that brilliant song.

It was a massive milestone in my career, but it wasn't actually a huge celebration for me. While the side strain, or the knee for that matter, hadn't bothered me too much during the game, we only had a short turnaround before the second Test in Hamilton. I'd had a taste of Test cricket and I wanted to make absolutely sure I was ready to go again. I had a couple of beers with the boys in the dressing-room after the game, but I didn't go overboard that night.

Cherie and Gav had to fly home, but Dad stayed on to catch up with me. I met Dad in the bar downstairs at the team hotel and it was great to chat about the past few days.

Brad Haddin came down and I introduced Dad to him. There was a team dinner on, but I wasn't sure whether family members were allowed so I hadn't asked Dad if he wanted to come along. He reckoned he was more than happy to go and find himself a feed at any of the many pubs around the place. Hadds asked him what he was doing for dinner and Dad told him he was going to wander off and find somewhere to eat, but Hadds wasn't having any of that ... 'Bullshit!' he said. 'You're having dinner with us.'

Dad didn't want to impose, but Dougie came down around then and he insisted that he come as well. I still wasn't sure what the protocol was, so when Ricky came down I had a quiet word and asked him how it went. Ricky's response was to walk straight over to Dad, introduce himself and tell him that he was coming to dinner with the team.

So there was my dad, with Ricky Ponting and Shane Watson to his left and Dougie Bollinger to his right ... he had the time of his life and I was so grateful for the way that the boys welcomed him and showed him a good time. It was a really special evening for me and Dad. And Dad was thrilled.

Gav wasn't too impressed, though, when Dad called him the next day to tell him he'd been rubbing shoulders with the entire Australian Test team.

* * *

Even though I had my baggy green and I'd done reasonably well in my Test debut, I told myself that I wouldn't consider myself to be a genuine Test player until I'd played ten Test matches—same as when I first made the one-day side.

I was determined not to be a one-Test wonder; having waited so long I wanted to play as much Test cricket as I possibly could while the opportunity was there in front of me.

I didn't think I was actually going to be in a position to play a second Test because I was certain the plane from Wellington to Hamilton wasn't going to make it. The airport had been closed because of high winds and had only reopened shortly before our flight took off. It was only a small twin-propeller aircraft and it really struggled. It's only about a 48-minute flight to Hamilton and I thought I was going to die for about 45 minutes of it. It was so bumpy; it was ridiculous.

I enjoy flying—I would have loved to have been a pilot if I was better at maths and physics at school—but that was the flight from hell. A few of the boys were using the vomit bags for most of the flight, but I was too scared to throw up. I nearly ripped the headrest in front of me off, I was hanging on so tight.

I didn't bat in Wellington. I was listed at No 11, which is a fair whack to the pride of any bowler. I was moved up to No 10 in Hamilton with Dougie Bollinger behind me, which is probably just as well because I think I would have retired immediately if Bollinger had gone in ahead of me!

We had another good win and celebrated taking out the series in fine style. I flew straight out to India from New Zealand for my second stint with the Deccan Chargers in the Indian Premier League. It was a long way to travel in one hit, but I appreciated the time to sit back and think about the past couple of months.

A lot had happened, most of it extremely positive, and I was grateful to have experienced it, but I promised myself I would leave no stone unturned in making sure this was the start of something bigger and not just that one great summer when I played for Australia.

CHAPTER 16

THE ASHES IN AUSTRALIA

My dream run came to a grinding halt at Lord's.

After a whirlwind summer with the national team and a short stint with Deccan, I was picked to go on the Australian tour of England and Ireland, which included a one-off ODI against Ireland, a five-game ODI series against England, and a two-Test series against Pakistan.

Pakistan wasn't playing any matches on home soil during that period due to security concerns and I was looking forward to adding to the two Tests I'd played in New Zealand. It was a real thrill to tour England with an Australian team despite it not being an Ashes series. It was a proud moment for me and it continued the wave of momentum my career was on at the time.

I always loved playing cricket in England regardless of what level it was at, but to go there and play for Australia was a dream come true. I was reasonably happy with how

I was bowling, a five-for in a 78-run win at The Oval was a highlight, but my knee was getting progressively worse throughout the tour.

Even after the troubles I had with it in the back half of 2009, I thought (probably naively) that it would eventually get better. But it started to dawn on me during that tour that this would be something I would need to manage for as long as I played.

We were disappointed to lose the first three games of the series, but we finished strongly to make it 3–2 on the back of the win at The Oval and a 42-run victory in the final match at Lord's. My knee had been really blowing up after games and Alex had to work overtime to keep me on the pitch.

My knee was sore, but manageable, but that changed when I went down to field off my own bowling late in the game at Lord's. I felt a sharp pain sear through the side of the knee. Thankfully it was late in the match, but it didn't take long for Alex to assess me and decide my tour was over.

I played at Lord's on 3 July 2010 and I was on David Young's operating table in Melbourne on 8 July. He repaired damage to my lateral meniscus (the cushioning material) and 'cleaned up' the joint. He also discovered I'd sustained reasonably significant cartilage damage to the outside compartment of my knee, which was new. He was also concerned about the onset of what he called 'bone edema', which basically meant that the two bones of my leg were rubbing up against each other in places where there was no cushioning material, which could start causing further damage.

None of that sounded good to me, but he assured me that I would be able to return to the Australian side after a decent recovery period and with careful management during a rehabilitation program. That part was music to my ears because England was heading to Australia for an Ashes series in November.

I wanted to play in that Ashes series so badly. I was determined to do everything I possibly could to put myself in a position to get picked. It was a challenging time. I'd bowl at training and be okay, but when I stepped up the intensity I hit trouble. My knee would blow up and I'd have to pull back a bit, which was the last thing I wanted to do.

I wore compression tubing on my knee to try to combat the swelling during that period, but after a while I started to feel like it locked the joint up and restricted my movement. I started to have to get it drained—it didn't happen too often back then—but that was something I struggled to get used to.

There's nothing too scientific about having fluid drained from your knee (or having the knee 'aspirated', as the docs call it); they just stick a bloody big needle in there and pull back on the syringe, which slowly fills up with a really gross yellow goo. I occasionally had it done in the dressing-room and a few of the boys would crowd around to have a look— only the bravest ones stuck around once that syringe started to fill up! It only takes 30 seconds or so and it really hurts, but it feels so much better after. It releases so much pressure.

I was getting regular injections into the knee with something called Synvisc—a substance partly made from chicken combs—which was meant to provide pain relief and act as a sort of artificial lubricant between the bones in my knee. That was effective for a while; but extended use can lead to side effects and that's exactly what happened with me.

After a course of injections my knee blew up like a balloon. I had the injections on the Friday afternoon of a long weekend, but it got so bad that I had to go and see a doctor on the holiday Monday to get a heap of fluid drained out of it. Not only was my knee huge, it was very, very painful!

It was a difficult time because, although I felt like Alex and David had a strong grasp on what was going on in my knee, there was still an element of trial and error in finding the best way to manage the issue so that I could stay on the field. It didn't matter what we did as far as I was concerned; if it was legal and there was even the slightest chance that it could help, then I was happy to try all kinds of treatment. I was on the cusp of playing in an Ashes series and there was no way I was going to let my knee stop me.

England had already been on Australian soil for a week when I played my first Sheffield Shield game in my comeback from that surgery in early November. The first Ashes Test started at the Gabba on 25 November so I knew I was up against it to prove my fitness.

I'd spoken with Alex Kountouris extensively in the lead-up to that Ashes series as we tried to plot the best way forward. He was constantly reassuring me that we'd done everything we possibly could, but even he admitted at one point that a leap of faith was required as far as my knee was concerned.

He basically said, 'If your knee goes—it goes—and we'll deal with it then.'

Either way, we'd sit down at the end of the Ashes series and work out whether it was going to be possible for me to continue playing Test-match cricket. With the damage I had sustained to the joint, there was a small chance that it could all end very quickly. I could bowl a ball, chip a piece of bone off and go down in a screaming heap and that would pretty much be it. I tried not to dwell on that scenario.

There were times when it didn't bother me too much and there were others when I'd wake up in the morning and not know how I was going to get through a day in the field, let alone bowl. But once I started to warm up and get some work into it I'd start to feel better.

I'd turned thirty-one by then and I really thought that Ashes series might have been my last chance to prove myself as a Test cricketer. I was determined to give it a really good crack and if that meant that my knee buckled under the strain then so be it. At least I'd know that I gave everything I had to try to fulfil my dream.

The Bulls had a big win over Tassie down at Bellerive and I pushed my case for a spot in the Australian team with 9 wickets for the match. I was stoked with the win and the good bowling figures, but I pulled up a bit sore and missed Queensland's next match against the Redbacks. I went to see David and he assured me this was normal. But it was enough for the Aussie selectors to rule me out of the first Test.

I was a bit down about it, but determined to bowl well again for the Bulls when they took on Victoria at the MCG. David had treated my knee with platelet-rich plasma (PRP) injections, which made me more comfortable. I managed 6 wickets in a drawn match that took place at the same time Australia and England fought out a draw in the first Test in Brisbane.

I got added to the Australian squad for the second Test in Adelaide on the last day of that Shield match. We were sitting in the dressing-room at the MCG after our match had finished when I got the call. It had been a tough six months since getting sent home from England, but the hard grind of rehab is all worth it when you get a call like that. To play in an Ashes Test in front of my friends and family at my old home ground in Adelaide was a dream come true.

I just sat there with a huge grin on my face. Queensland skipper James Hopes had a pretty good idea what had just happened and he came over and shook my hand. The rest of the boys quickly cottoned on and they were all rapt for me, which was nice.

When I think of the Ashes I think about sitting with Mum, Dad and Gav and watching players like Steve and Mark Waugh, David Boon, Shane Warne, Glenn McGrath—all legends of the game through a golden era of Australian cricket. I just think there is no purer form of the game. It's fair to say that I arrived at Adelaide Oval on the first day of my first Ashes Test with a spring in my step. My buoyant mood didn't last long, though.

Ricky Ponting won the toss and we had a bat, but we made a shocking start. Simon Katich, Punter and Michael Clarke were dismissed in quick succession and we were 2–3 after about ten minutes of play.

Mike Hussey and Shane Watson steadied the ship with a partnership of 94, but we were all out for 245 late in the evening session on day one. To my great embarrassment I made a first-ball duck, but more on that later.

The changeover between innings happened so late that we only got 1 over in before stumps. Ricky threw me the ball. I was fired up, as you can imagine, but the significance of opening the bowling for Australia against England at Adelaide Oval wasn't lost on me. I'd bowled well against Pakistan at my old home ground back in January, but this was something else.

I strayed onto the legs of Andrew Strauss with my first ball and they took a single leg bye, but Alastair Cook was content to defend the over and get into the dressing-room.

Dougie Bollinger, who came into the side for the second Test with me at the expense of Mitch Johnson and Ben Hilfenhaus, struck early when he bowled Strauss in the first over on day two, but it was a rare moment of joy for us. England finished that day at 2–317, and batted into the fourth day before declaring at 5–620 in the morning session.

It was a fairly traditional Adelaide wicket, which was quite batsman-friendly, but as bowlers we didn't stick to the plans we had in place nearly well enough.

The top order batted well to see us finish the day at 4–238, with rain starting to become a factor; but we faced a big task to bat out the fifth day to salvage a draw.

But Huss went early on the final day and it all went downhill from there.

I went in after Hadds edged one to the keeper off Jimmy Anderson. After getting out first ball in the first innings I was facing a king pair, but that was the last thing on my mind.

I was determined to do what I could to keep our rearguard action going.

Of course, it didn't work out like that. Facing Anderson I left one and it hit me on the pads. Jimmy was absolutely on fire and swinging the ball both ways. I thought that it had hit me quite high so I referred it to DRS (Decision Review System), which showed it was going to hit middle and leg about halfway up—which was embarrassing to say the least. I copped grief from teammates about that referral years later.

Back then we probably didn't deal with DRS as well as some other teams. We ultimately figured out a more effective approach that included conferring with the non-striker before sending a decision for referral.

I was so angry and disgusted with myself. I absolutely destroyed my bat when I got back into the rooms. I'm not one to have massive temper tantrums as a rule—it's not really a great look—but I was so pissed off with myself after I got out that I let rip. Unfortunately, it was my beautiful County bat that copped it as I used it like a lumberjack's axe on the floor!

Mostly I was disappointed that I hadn't done my bit to help the side save the match. But I was also angry because I wasn't actually out in the first innings. I was given out LBW, but I hit the ball—smacked it actually. It wasn't the best shot to try to get off the mark, but I nicked it onto my back pad and the umpire gave me out. Before I could refer it to the third umpire, Brad Haddin had already done it from the non-striker's end because he'd seen and heard me hit the ball.

All the fielders went up, and as we stood around I heard someone say that he thought I'd nicked it as well. I was feeling safe as we stood around and waited for the decision, but I was absolutely dumbfounded when the call came down that I was still out.

I was fuming as I walked off and my mood wasn't helped when I got back into the dressing-room and they were showing the mark the ball clearly made on my bat on the television. To make matters worse, it was later explained to us that the reason the third umpire couldn't see the nick on the replay was because he didn't have a high-definition television! I was absolutely spewing.

I'm pretty sure I'd never got a golden duck in any form of cricket and to get two in two innings in a Test match against England in front of my family and friends was hugely embarrassing! That disappointment didn't come close to what I felt for the team, though. With rain forecast, we just couldn't put together a partnership and went down by an innings and 71 runs before lunch.

I was already in getting a scan on a minor shoulder muscle tear I'd picked up on day three when the storm hit around lunchtime. It bucketed down for the rest of the afternoon and would have certainly saved us had we been able to dig in better.

I'd picked up an injury, but Simon Katich had fared even worse. He was struggling with an Achilles injury going into the match and it got a lot worse on him during that Test. He was really hobbling between wickets and it was shattering when he was ruled out for the rest of the summer. He worked so hard to try to play through it, but the pain just got too much. He was a tough bugger, Kat. I only got to play a handful of games with him, but I really respected the way he went about his cricket.

England hadn't won a series in Australia for a long time, but we had great respect for them as a team. Even so we had high expectations of our own performances and we didn't compete at the level required in Adelaide. The Poms played really well, everything seemed to click for them, whereas we struggled to find our rhythm as a group. I thought we planned really well for them.

We had specific plans for all of their batsmen. For example, we knew Alastair Cook and Jonathan Trott were both really strong off their pads, but we didn't stick to those plans as a bowling attack. Too often we strayed onto their legs and we paid the price. Ricky made it clear what the plan was, but we just continued to bowl too straight.

I have had a bit of success against Cook since that series and it's only because I've heeded that advice and bowled more of a fourth-stump line.

We just didn't get it right—perhaps it was us being a bit selfish and going for the glory ball on the stumps. I thought I was bowling in the right spot, but looking back on it I was way too straight.

The rooms were pretty sombre after that loss. Representing our country is what we're about and we felt we'd let a lot of people down with that performance. You can't dwell on a performance like that though; it's about pinpointing what went wrong, figuring out how to address that issue, and getting back to work.

That series was a big learning curve for me in terms of media coverage because it was the first time I'd been part of a struggling Australian team. It was the first time I'd picked up the paper and read strong criticism of the team. I accept that criticism comes with poor performances, but some of the stuff that was written about the team, and Ricky in particular, was way off the mark. I felt given what he'd done for Australian cricket over a long period of time that Ricky deserved the benefit of the doubt, but the press went after him mercilessly.

He was the same old Ricky around the team, though. He was hitting the ball really well in the nets and I felt it was only a matter of time before he made some runs. You wouldn't have thought he was under siege by the media with the way he carried on behind the scenes.

After a massive defeat like that I don't think many of the bowlers felt confident of keeping their spot in the side. But the skipper was happy enough with how I bowled and I held my spot for the trip to Perth for the third Test.

It's the lot of the fast bowler really; sometimes you feel like you're bowling really well and get no reward and other times you feel like you're bowling rubbish and you'll take five-for. The key for me is to try to minimise the gap between my best and worst.

Mike Hussey wanted the team to stay together and have a dinner after the Adelaide loss, but most of the boys had already booked flights home because we had a decent break until the Perth Test. He felt it was important that we stick together, but too many guys had travel plans they couldn't change. I stayed in Adelaide to have dinner with some friends and I actually caught up with him later for a few beers.

Huss taught me a lot about what it means to be a part of the Australian cricket team; he was a player who really set the tone in terms of team culture. I'd respected him from afar long before I'd made it into the Australian team, so to be able to share some time with him was great.

* * *

We were keen to get to Perth because its pace and bounce traditionally made it a difficult environment for visiting England teams, while our batsmen generally enjoyed the conditions. But we were in all sorts at 5–69 on the first day after being sent in to bat. Mike Hussey and Brad Haddin both made half-centuries, though, and the tail (excluding me!) wagged and we made it to 268.

Mitch Johnson had come back into the side and top-scored for us with 62. I think this might have boosted his confidence because he produced an inspired spell of bowling in the Poms' first dig. He hadn't enjoyed a great start to the series, but the WACA wicket suited him down to the ground. He'd worked really hard in the nets in Adelaide and I felt he was primed for a big showing. He'd had issues with accuracy early in the summer, but his pace was still right up there.

They were getting away from us at 0–78 on the second day and Mitch just turned it on. At one stage he'd taken 4–7 as he ripped through the England top order. Punter hit the nail on the head when he called it 'one of the all-time great Ashes spells'. Mitch was getting the ball to come back in at the batsman and, with his pace, it made him near unplayable at times. It was a hell of a spell of fast bowling.

When he's bowling like that it's important for the bowler at the other end, whoever it is, to be very disciplined with line and length to keep building pressure. If that's me then I won't necessarily get the wickets in that scenario, but I will have done my job for the team if I keep the runs down from my end.

Mitch might end up with 5–20 and I might bowl 15 overs for 30 runs, but I'll be happy that I've done my job. It's the same for all the bowlers; we're not just plugging away separately at either end ... we work together to achieve the team goal. It's a lot like batting partnerships in that sense.

One day Mitch Johnson or Peter Siddle might get 5 or 6 wickets, but other days it will be me or Ben Hilfenhaus or Dougie Bollinger or Nathan Lyon. We try to impress that on the younger bowlers when they come in: bowling can seem like a pretty solitary pursuit, but to win matches you need a team approach; you need to combine well together as a unit.

We bowled them out for 187 and were better with the bat in our second innings. Shane Watson was unlucky not to make a ton, out for 95, but Mike Hussey fared better to score his second century of the series. I only made one lousy run, but I had the privilege to be out there with Huss when he cracked triple figures.

Above: Deccan Chargers captain, Adam Gilchrist, receives the trophy from the South African president, Jacob Zuma, after we won the 2009 IPL Twenty20 final in South Africa.

Below: An amazing moment with the Deccan Chargers, meeting the Dalai Lama.

Above: A fair old outing at the WACA during the fourth ODI against Pakistan in January 2010, the old scoreboard telling a happy tale for me.

Below: One of the celebrations during that haul at the WACA; Punter, Shaun Marsh and Pup were happy to share the love that night.

Above: A special moment after I was presented with my baggy green cap by Ricky Ponting on my Test debut in New Zealand in March 2010.

Below: Andrew Strauss checks to see just how much damage has been done from my short ball collecting Kevin Pietersen in an ODI at Old Trafford in June 2010.

Above: Great catch low down by Steve Smith to remove Paul Collingwood off the last ball of the day against England during the Third Test at the WACA during the 2010 Ashes series.

Below: Phil Hughes and I doing our best to keep Ricky's spirits up as he was fighting to overcome a broken finger in order to play in the Boxing Day Test against the Poms in the Fourth Test of the 2010 Ashes series.

Above: Ricky made it onto the field … but that was the end of me as my ankle collapsed during the Fourth Test.

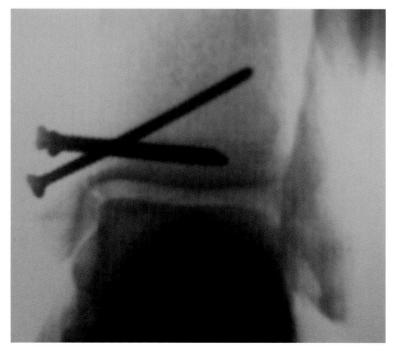

Left: An X-ray of my ankle after it was pinned back together.

Above: Into my stride and searching for English wickets at the WACA during the 2013 Ashes series, a Test we were always going to back ourselves to win.

Below: If anyone deserved a beer to cool down after winning that Test match it was Mitch!

Above: Feeling absolutely zero pain after taking the last wicket in our hard fought third Test victory over South Africa at Sahara Park Newlands in 2014.

Below: Celebrating the end of an amazing series against South Africa in 2014, and a gratifying twelve months for Australian cricket.

Above: A perfect day in every way— our wedding day.

Right: Commentating on the cricket in October 2014, while recovering from the knee op.

I'd never been out in the middle when a teammate had made a hundred in a Test. What an experience it was to be out there when the great Mr Cricket himself scored his thirteenth Test ton. I'd seen similar scenes on television so many times, but to be out there and hear the roar of the crowd and share that moment with him was really special. It was a massive innings in the context of a match we absolutely had to win.

We set them a target of 391 and they didn't get close.

I was a little bit expensive early, which is never ideal, but I always look on that as a bit of a test of character. It's easy to drop your head and think that it's just not going to be your day—I've certainly been guilty of that in the past—but there are few things more satisfying than digging deep and fighting back with a few wickets.

A five-for in a Test is special for any bowler, but for me to grab 6 wickets in an Ashes Test victory was a proud moment. Matt Prior was my fifth wicket; it bounced a bit on him from just short of a length and Huss took the catch at gully.

It was a great feeling and it was nice to be able to share that with the boys and Huss, in particular, after I'd been there for his big moment. I must admit I made sure I took a moment to soak it up as I held the ball up to the WACA crowd.

It got even better when Steven Finn edged one off my next over to Steve Smith at third slip to give us the win.

Winning a Test match is a bloody hard thing to do. The veteran guys like Ricky and Huss always used to say that we had to celebrate a Test win because you never know when the next one is going to come. I certainly found that to be true and it was great to sit back with the boys in the rooms having squared the series at 1–1.

* * *

I'd always wondered what Christmas Day was like for the Australian cricket team given so many of the boys were away from home. I've always loved Christmas and I wasn't sure what to expect heading into the Boxing Day Test, but I was pleasantly surprised. All the boys flew their families in, if they weren't travelling with them already through Cricket Australia, and Crown Casino put on a great lunch.

There was a training session on the MCG in the morning, which was optional, but most of the boys turned up. It was quite surreal to be out there on that hallowed turf in that marvellous, and empty, stadium a day before it would be filled with 80 or 90,000 fans. It was a very light session and those guys with kids brought them out onto the grass for a muck-around afterwards, which was great.

Back at Crown there was a room set up with a brilliant buffet and a separate room for all the kids to play with toys and video games. It was a really enjoyable day for me and Cherie, but it certainly wasn't a late one with one of the biggest days on the cricket calendar looming.

The bounce and pace at the WACA is almost unique in world cricket and England didn't handle the conditions well. Perhaps we should have taken that into account when assessing the win. Maybe we took a little too much confidence from the performance ... because they absolutely brained us in Melbourne.

Having sent us in, England bowled us out for an embarrassing 98. Then they set about retaining the Ashes with the bat. Cook and Strauss put on 159 for the first wicket before both were dismissed in quick succession, but then Trott and Pietersen pushed the score past 250.

I was part of a controversial incident a few overs after lunch on the second day when I bowled to KP and Brad Haddin appealed loudly for a catch. I didn't go up initially because I didn't hear anything, but Hadds was adamant, so Ricky sent it to review.

There was a little scratch on Hot Spot, but it was about 10 cm away from where the ball passed the bat, so umpire Aleem Dar's initial call of 'not out' stood.

Ricky had broken a bone in the little finger on his left hand over in Perth, which would have sidelined most players, but he was as tough as they come and there was no way he was missing a Boxing Day Test with the Ashes on the line.

I think the frustration and pressure of the summer boiled over for Punter a bit at that point—he's since admitted as much—but we were all frustrated with the DRS by then. It had been so inconsistent—for both teams—and we just wanted a bit more consistency. KP wandered over and said that he'd hit it, even though he thought he hadn't, just to stir the pot a bit.

Punter pushed his case for a while with both umpires, to the point he was fined 40 per cent of his match fee. I felt bad that we'd allowed ourselves to even be in that position to start with.

The Poms went on to make 513, but I didn't see out the innings.

I had a bit of soreness in my left ankle going into the Test, but I'd recently gone from boots to lower-cut shoes, so I put it down to that. I'd trained in them for a couple of days and they felt fine until I started to develop a bit of soreness the day before the Test. I changed back to my boots. I'd only decided to try the shoes because the manufacturer was going to stop making the boots. The soreness seemed to go away.

But the pain came back and got worse as the second day wore on. I tried another pair of boots that I'd worn in already and they felt okay, but towards the end of the second day I was in a fair bit of pain when I bowled.

The doc injected a bit of local anaesthetic into it and I iced it overnight. I went for a scan on the morning of the third day and they injected cortisone in there to help with inflammation. The scan didn't show anything and with the injections on board I felt good again.

At one point on the third day I told Ricky how good it was feeling. Two balls later it happened ... CRACK!

Mitch Johnson reckoned he heard my ankle break from where he was fielding in the covers.

I was about three steps away from going into my bowling action when I felt it go. I pulled up as quickly as I could and went to ground. It was a strange feeling because it didn't really hurt that much. I knew something was badly wrong, but the local anaesthetic and the cortisone were still present in my ankle, so I got up and tried to walk around a bit.

I took the boot off and had a look at it, but I couldn't see anything wrong. Clearly something was amiss, though, so I hobbled off and they took me straight back to the place where I'd been scanned earlier that day.

This time the evidence was clear. You didn't have to be a doctor to see the fracture line through the bone. When David Young saw it he told me it was a decent break. Part of the inside knuckle of my ankle—the medial malleolus—had snapped clean off.

It had nothing to do with my choice of shoes. I'd played a lot of cricket in the lead-up to that Test and the workload going through that ankle had built up to the point where something gave way. It didn't show up on the initial scans, but they don't always pick up low-grade stress reactions.

Back at the ground I lay down in the physio room and didn't move for about two hours. I was absolutely shattered. All the boys were really disappointed for me and tried to get around me as much as they could, but what can you say to someone in that situation?

After the dramas with my knee I had felt like I was finally starting to make some real progress at international level. It was still sore, but we were managing it, and my confidence in our approach was growing.

To have something completely out of the blue happen like that was a bitter pill to swallow, to put it mildly. At my age the smallest setback could end my career, but this was a huge one.

Worse was to come, though. With all of those negative thoughts swirling around in my head, the local anaesthetic started to wear off and I found myself in the most excruciating pain I'd ever felt.

Alex initially told me that the fact I'd been able to walk off the ground under my own steam was a positive sign, but it gave us false hope. With the painkillers out of my system, I was left in no doubt whatsoever that this was a serious injury.

Even so, I pondered finding a way to bat in our second innings, but we were so far behind that we never seriously considered it.

Early on the fourth day we lost the Test by an innings and 157 runs and England retained the Ashes. I was on David Young's operating table again that afternoon. He inserted two big screws into the ankle, which he assured me would fix the issue, but there would be a lengthy recovery period.

I was laid up in Melbourne for two or three days then flew back up to Brisbane to lie on the couch and feel sorry for myself. Cherie was great and looked after me, despite me being a horrible patient.

Cricket Australia put out a release saying that I'd miss three to four months, but there was no way I was going to be out for that long. I did sook it up a bit early, but it wasn't long before I hardened up and decided to get back as soon as I could.

Still, I was really disappointed to miss the rest of the Australian summer. The World Cup in India and Sri Lanka was only a couple of months away as well, so there was no way I'd be ready for that. I'd had a good run in the one-dayers and I really wanted to make that squad and represent my country at a World Cup.

Like anything in life, though, in the face of adversity you can either curse your luck and feel sorry for yourself or you can accept what's happened and go about fixing it. That only happens with hard work. I quickly set myself a few goals and set about putting together a rehab program.

My biggest concern was the position of the fracture. It's estimated that a fast bowler puts about eight times his body weight through his front foot in the delivery stride. In my mind there was a weakness in that ankle now, so how on earth was I ever going to bowl with anything like the intensity I'd managed before the break?

David quickly allayed those fears. He said that with the screws in there it should actually be stronger than it previously was. Once it had healed properly it was just a matter of gradually increasing my training workload and, perhaps more importantly, slowly regaining confidence in my bowling action.

Sure enough, the psychological aspect of recovery was the area I found most challenging. I'd put myself through plenty of gruelling rehab programs before—too many—so the physical aspect was no problem. It was hard work, of course, but I was always confident that if I did the work I'd achieve the desired result at the end of the process. With this break there were nagging doubts, despite the assurances of David and Alex.

I visited David in Melbourne in early February for a check-up on my ankle. He was happy with how it was healing but, to add insult to injury, he determined that my knee needed further surgery. It had been grumbling along that summer, but the increased load of three (well, two and a half) Tests had taken a toll. I underwent a fifth arthroscopic procedure on my right knee, with David cleaning out several loose bodies that had been causing me ongoing pain.

It was a setback I clearly didn't need in terms of my return to the Australian side, which was my main focus. But there were potentially dire financial ramifications for me too. I had been picked up by Indian Premier League side Kings XI Punjab at the IPL auction in January. If I couldn't get back on my feet and bowling in time for the League's early April kick-off, then one of the biggest contracts of my career would be torn up.

CHAPTER 17

THE SHORT GAME

I enjoy playing Twenty20 cricket, even though it's meant to be a slogfest for batsmen.

It's good fun to be able to go out there in front of big crowds and put on a bit of a show. As a bowler, I like the challenge of coming up with different variations and different fields to try to combat the big hitting.

There's a commonly held belief that the rise of the shortest form of the game will slowly erode the popularity of one-day and Test cricket, but I don't subscribe to that theory. I think the experimentation that T20 allows has had really positive flow-on effects for the other forms of cricket. From a batting perspective, scoring in ODIs and Tests is a lot quicker these days and I think T20 has a fair bit to do with that.

We took a while to get on board the Twenty20 train in Australia. There were plenty of people who thought it might be a fad early on, which wasn't helped with party tricks such as Andrew Johns playing a couple of games for New South Wales back in 2007. Great Rugby League player, but you've got to earn the cap!

The Poms may have invented it, but it's probably fair to say that India is the country that's really taken the ball and ran with it. The Indian Premier League has been wildly successful since its first season in 2008 and I was fortunate enough to experience it firsthand.

There's no denying it has proven to be a huge financial windfall for a lot of international cricketers too. When Kings XI Punjab successfully bid for me at the 2011 IPL auction the successful bid was US$325,000 ... and I had a broken ankle at the time! There are terms and conditions that come with that, of course. Basically, what that meant was I would go to play for Kings for roughly that amount of money per IPL season for two years with an option for a third.

I was out at a dinner with Cherie when Dad called me and told me that Kings had successfully bid for me. It's fair to say I ordered a nice bottle of wine to go with our food that night. But that figure was actually at the lower end of what players were getting paid that year.

David Hussey and Adam Gilchrist were Punjab's two big signings that year—they went for US$1.4 million and US$900,000 respectively.

Kings XI Punjab was my second IPL team. My first season in the competition was in 2009 when Darren Lehmann got me to play for Deccan Chargers. Boof had just taken over as coach and the whole franchise was basically starting from scratch after they finished last in the first season of the IPL the year before.

They brought in Adam Gilchrist to captain the side and had big names such as Andrew Symonds, VVS Laxman, Herschelle Gibbs and Chaminda Vaas. I wasn't expecting to get much of a look in, to be honest.

Boof had got me over as an uncapped player (I hadn't made my international ODI debut yet), which meant that I didn't go through the auction—I wouldn't have got picked up if I'd gone that way. I signed a two-year deal, which was a lot more modest than my Kings contract two years later. At the time I was just keen to learn what I could from some of those stars and gain some experience at a really high level.

I was keen to get to know all of my teammates as much as I could because it is a bit of a challenge to gel together as a team when a bunch of players are thrown together from all over the world. That's where Boof and Gilly excelled. They're both personable sorts of characters who are easy to get to know and are very inclusive. A few of the younger Indian fellas were a bit in awe of Gilly at the start, but they quickly realised that he valued what they brought to the team and was keen to make sure they performed as well as possible.

That series was held in South Africa because there were security concerns in India at the time. It was great to see a bit of the country. We were well looked after and stayed in beautiful hotels everywhere we went.

As it turned out I did get an opportunity in the back half of the series when West Indies quick Fidel Edwards had to leave because the Windies were going on tour in England.

It took me a little while to find my feet, but Boof stuck with me and I took 3 wickets in the semifinal, which I hoped went some way to repaying his faith in me.

After falling into that semifinal—we lost our last two group games and squeaked in on net run rate—we played really well and beat the Delhi Daredevils, who had finished on top of the table. It was a huge deal for some of these big-name players who'd been around for ages to make it into the final. As you can imagine, I was pumped to get a chance at an IPL champions title.

I know some detractors look at the big money on offer and think that everyone's just over there for a pay cheque and that it doesn't really matter to the players. But when you get a bunch of elite cricketers together it could be a game in the park and we could be playing for sheep stations. We worked hard together to establish a good team bond and we were hell bent on getting a win.

We played Royal Challengers Bangalore at Wanderers Stadium in Johannesburg in front of a huge crowd. Anyone who was there that night would know how much it meant to the players. Gilly had been braining them with the bat all season, he ended up taking Player of the Series honours, but he was out in the first over for a duck.

We didn't bat well apart from Herschelle Gibbs, who anchored the innings with 53 not out. We struggled to 143 off our 20 overs. The crowd was already loud after every delivery, but the noise level went up every time we took a wicket.

I opened the bowling and was pleased to concede just one leg bye. It was Simmo and Indian left-armer Pragyan Ojha who did the damage for us. Gilly effected two stumpings as well, and we were still right in it when I came on to bowl the second-to-last over.

They needed 27 off 12 balls and I went for 12 before Harmeet Singh took a brilliant catch running in from fine leg to dismiss Vinay Kumar off my last ball.

RP Singh bowled a brilliant over at the death and the crowd went nuts when he kept them to just 8 runs to seal Deccan's first-ever IPL win. They were great scenes and there was a lot of emotion as the rest of the team charged the field from the dugout. I was there with a core of Aussies, but I really think every player appreciated how everyone had pulled together as a team.

Despite that success it probably wasn't until I got to India for my second season that I realised how truly massive the IPL is over there. They hated that it was in South Africa in 2009 and loved having it back on home soil. They're just such fanatical cricket fans, which is great, but it also meant I couldn't walk down the street without stacks of people coming up to me and wanting a photo or an autograph or just to chat. That's fine when it's one or two people at a time, but it was a lot more than that when I did make the mistake of going outside the hotel on my own.

It was quite overwhelming for me because I never really got recognised as a cricket player back home. Even later in my career when I'd played in a few Ashes series, I could sit in a cafe with Cherie and I might only get one or two people give me a nod and say g'day. I like my personal space, but it seemed like everyone knew who I was over there. The organisers don't actually like you going out on your own because you could get mobbed.

There were lots of little things I had to think about in India, which I had never had to consider before. Security was definitely one of them, but another was being quite vigilant about what you eat and where you eat it from. The hotels we stayed in generally catered for my Western tastes, but it's almost inevitable that you'll get crook guts from eating something not quite right at some point. I had that happen to me in my first IPL season and it's definitely not pleasant. It's certainly not conducive to fast bowling!

I'm not quite as bad as Warnie packing tins of baked beans to eat while I'm on tour, though. I did try a bit of the local food and let me tell you it was the hottest thing I've ever tasted. I don't mind a little bit of heat, but this grub was positively volcanic!

Unfortunately, you also have to be very careful who you talk to about cricket. We were always warned about the strict anti-corruption rules they have over there, but it didn't stop a few players getting into trouble during my time in the IPL. There are harsh bans as a strong deterrent to any sort of betting activity. I have absolutely no problem with that because the integrity of the game should never, ever be put in a position where it can be called into question.

I never had anyone approach me like that over there and if I had I would have reported it immediately, but you do have to be extremely careful. Betting on cricket is massive over there and you can get yourself in trouble just by inadvertently saying the wrong thing to the wrong person. If people want to have a chat then I'm happy to, but I'm always wary of anyone who's too interested in particular aspects of the game.

Even in my second year at Deccan we couldn't play at our home ground in Hyderabad because there were still security risks in that area. We had to use various other home grounds, which was a bit disappointing because I didn't get that feeling of being the home team. Nagpur was one of the main ones.

The security concerns are very real over there, though, as we saw when two small bombs went off outside an IPL game in Bangalore late in the series. We made the semi-finals that year and were due to play at the same stadium a few days later, but they moved both semis to Mumbai because of the threat of further terrorist action.

It's a shame there is that aspect to playing cricket in India, because it's an amazing place.

We got knocked out in that semifinal by Chennai Super Kings. Then I went into the auction in 2011, where Kings XI Punjab picked me up because my two-year deal with the Chargers was finished.

Boof was still the coach at Deccan that year and he was keen to have me back, but the owners had also made it clear that they wanted to bring South African quick Dale Steyn in as well. The IPL auction is just like a yearling sale where they sell horses to the highest bidder—except it's cricketers that go under the auctioneer's hammer. Given his status in world cricket, Dale was a big-ticket item that year and it cost Deccan US$1.2 million to get him to the franchise.

He was the player who was auctioned just before me, so Deccan had done their dough and didn't have the budget to bid for me too. Kings XI Punjab had finished last in 2010 and they brought in Adam Gilchrist to try to turn things around in 2011. Gilly and I had really enjoyed playing together at Deccan and he convinced the owners at Kings to bid for me even though I was coming back from the ankle fracture I suffered in the Boxing Day Test.

I'm glad he did because it was a whole new experience to play for Kings, who were based way up in the north of the country near the mountains. They split their home games between Mohali and Dharamsala, which is even further north and is about 1500 metres above sea level.

Dharamsala is the home of His Holiness the Dalai Lama, the Tibetan government in exile and one of the most stunning cricket grounds on the planet. It's a very open ground with one covered grandstand, but the main feature is the snow-capped mountains you can see off in the distance from most points of the ground.

It's quite a peaceful, spiritual place; it's a bit of a mecca for yoga and Pilates types as well, which only adds to that vibe. I actually got to meet the Dalai Lama when I was still with Deccan when we played Kings there in 2010. It was a just a quick meet and greet, but he definitely has a presence about him.

It was an amazing place to play cricket. It's an amazing place to have a beer at the end of a season too. We played Deccan there in the last game of the 2011 series and neither of us made the finals that year. Boof was still with Deccan at that stage, so Gilly, a few of the lads and I went a bit further up the hill to a good spot with a great view and a few bars.

I don't know when we lost Boof, but Gilly and I watched the sun come up at the end of that session. We were drinking herbal tea by then and a herd of goats wandered past with the mountains on one side and the valley on the other—truly one of the most surreal moments of my life!

I don't remember a lot of our conversation at that point in proceedings, but I daresay we'd probably taken the opportunity to convene a quick meeting of the 'King Pair Club' at some stage. Gilly was chairman of the club, having made his pair of golden ducks against India in Calcutta in 2001, and I joined him in the exclusive club after my efforts in the Adelaide Test in the Ashes series of 2010. We both reckon we were terribly harshly done by in the manner of our first dismissals, so we had a lot of common ground for discussion.

Boof came over to coach Kings from 2012, but we never quite recaptured the form that took us to the 2009 title. I played thirteen games for Kings in 2011, which was my biggest IPL season by five matches. I only managed eight in 2012 and then three in 2013, due to an Australian tour of the West Indies and an Achilles injury respectively.

It's always about getting the result when I play cricket anywhere, but I found the IPL, in its timing on the calendar and length, also gave me an excellent opportunity to try a few different things with my bowling. Ultimately, that helped me develop as a bowler.

I met some great people and it was always a little surreal to be playing against fellow Australians in front of those heaving crowds in some exotic places.

India is a wonderful, if at times confronting, place and I enjoyed my time in the Indian Premier League immensely. Cricket tours aside, I'm not much of a world traveller and it's probably a place I never would have got to experience if left to my own devices. I'm glad cricket allowed me to get to know the country a bit.

* * *

I was always keen to put my hand up to play Twenty20 cricket for Australia, but I don't think the selectors ever really saw me as someone who had a future in that side. I played three Twenty20 games for Australia when I was enjoying a bit of an ODI rebirth in the first half of 2010, but that was pretty much it.

There are probably a couple of quite valid reasons for that. First, it's a fairly young man's game at international level and I think it's a great format for some of our up-and-coming bowlers to showcase what they can do. Second, the Aussie selectors knew all too well what it took to get me on the park some days. With the amount of cricket that gets played these days it's difficult for anyone to play regularly across all three forms of the game—let alone an old fella with a grumpy knee like me!

I initially had mixed feelings about the move away from the state team format in our domestic T20 competition.

Playing for that state cap is important in all forms of the game, but I must admit I've been really impressed with how the Big Bash League has taken off since it came in with city-based teams.

There is a lot more chopping and changing of players between teams, so it does lose that element of pride in representing your state colours, but I think it fits nicely into the Australian cricket calendar.

Unfortunately, I haven't been able to play a lot of cricket for my team, the Brisbane Heat, because of national duties or injury. But I was still thrilled when the boys managed to claim BBL02. I hope the concept keeps gaining momentum because I think it's good for Australian cricket.

CHAPTER 18

TRYING TIMES AND MAROON MAGIC

I laid down a solid foundation for an international career over the Australian summer of 2009–10 but, despite my best efforts, I wasn't able to build on that foundation as quickly as I would have liked.

The broken ankle at the Boxing Day Test was an obvious momentum stopper, but there were more challenges to come.

It took a lot of hard work to recover in time from that fracture—and the arthroscope I had on my knee a month later—in time to start my first IPL season with Kings XI Punjab. I was really pleased with the amount of cricket I was able to play for Kings that year and felt that it put me back on the right track.

I was picked to go on the tour of Sri Lanka, which started with a couple of T20 matches then rolled into five ODIs and finished with a three-Test series. Given my injury history and my multitude of conversations with Alex, I always knew that I would need to focus on one form of cricket at some point.

There was never a clear directive that this was happening, but it started to become clear to me around that time that the Australian selectors felt Test cricket was where I was best utilised.

I love Test cricket, but given the demands it places on your body over five days, I'd always thought my future was in the short, sharp formats of ODIs or T20s. But as long as I played for my country I was happy.

I didn't get a look-in while the T20s and the ODI series were on. Sri Lanka took the Twenty20 series 2–0 and the boys won a hard-fought ODI series 3–2.

The first Test was in Galle, which is a beautiful ground by the ocean right down the south of Sri Lanka. It was devastated by the Boxing Day tsunami in 2004, but they did a lot of work to restore it to its former glory after that tragic disaster. It meant a lot to me to visit there.

In purely cricketing terms, it was also significant for a couple of reasons: it was Michael Clarke's first Test since taking over from Ricky Ponting as captain and it was Nathan Lyon's Test debut.

It turned out well for both of them, with Pup making a half-century in the second innings of a 125-run win, and Nathan Lyon getting a wicket with his first ball in Test cricket, then going on to snare a five-for.

To put the cherry on top for Nathan, he took the wicket of their best batsman in Kumar Sangakkara and took a classic catch off his own bowling for his fifth wicket. You wouldn't read about it ...

It was significant for me, too, because I needed a good performance under my belt to re-establish myself in the side. I was really pleased to snag a five-for in the second innings.

It was a bit different with Pup in charge, but I thought the transition from Ricky to Michael was as smooth as we could have hoped for. Punter had endured a tough summer, physically and mentally, and decided to step down from the captaincy to concentrate on his batting and enjoying the game more after the World Cup. I knew Michael was ready to step in and would do a good job, but I also knew that Punter had a lot left to give to the game and they'd be able to work well together.

It was about a three-and-a-half hour drive from Galle to Pallekele, where the second Test was held, but we actually got there via seaplane, which was a bit of a novelty. It's a picturesque part of the world and that was a great way to get a good look at it.

We'd done well to get a result out of Galle because the weather was atrocious, but we didn't have the same luck in Pallekele. The Sri Lankans were better with the bat in the second innings after we bowled them out for 174 in the first, then the combination of bad light and rain did the rest.

Despite my extensive history of injuries I'd never had many soft tissue problems, but I strained a hamstring late in that Test. I didn't think it was too bad at the time, but I wasn't right for the third test in Colombo and I was sent home.

That third match also ended in a draw, which gave us a rare series win on the Subcontinent.

It was enough to keep me out of the third Test in Sri Lanka, but my hamstring injury wasn't severe and I was able to join the squad for a short tour of South Africa in October and November.

I wasn't part of the squad that won the ODI series 2–1, but I was included for the first Test in Cape Town, which turned out to be one of the more bizarre cricket experiences of my life.

We had a 188-run lead after we bowled them out for 96 in their first innings—we had them on the ropes—then we got skittled for 47 in our second innings. You see two scores like that and assume that the wicket is going nuts—it was doing a bit, but there wasn't enough in it to suggest it could see two sides bowled out for less than a hundred each. Michael Clarke had batted his way to 151 in the first innings and both teams combined couldn't pass his mark in the next two digs!

It was embarrassing for all of us to be involved in an innings of 47, but it was just one of those situations where wickets fell early and the rest were like dominoes. You walk to the crease knowing you need to dig in, but that's probably the wrong mindset.

Watto had done the business in the South African batting collapse with 5 wickets and I provided some support with 4. It's enjoyable when you see it happening to the opposition but not nearly as much when you're sitting in the dressing-room watching the wickets tumble.

We lost the match by 8 wickets and I hurt myself … again.

I'd had what David Young called 'unhappy' hips for a while, but I aggravated my right hip bowling in South Africa's second innings. Technically speaking, I had inflammation in both sacroiliac joints and femoroacetabular impingements on both sides. It's something AFL players get a bit, and it causes pain at and around where the leg bones meet the pelvis. Like most fast bowlers I also had an ongoing L5-S1 issue called spondylolisthesis where the L5 disc at the bottom of my spine is pushed further forward than it should be in relation to my pelvic bone. There was a bit going on down there!

All of that had been manageable up to that point, but I pulled up very sore after that Test.

I was okay in my bowling action, but I couldn't get any momentum running in to the crease. The pain felt really deep in my pelvis. They tried, but failed, to jab it up with a bit of local anaesthetic. It was only a short break before the next Test in Johannesburg. I just couldn't get up in time, so I was on the plane home early again.

I hated to leave another tour, but I was pleased to see Patty Cummins come in and do so well in his Test debut. Pat took 6 wickets in the second innings to claim player of the match honours in a 2-wicket comeback win by the boys.

We discussed the possibility of surgery on my hips, but Alex was reluctant because he'd seen some indifferent results in cricketers who went down that path. We decided to continue managing it with a combination of targeted exercise, manipulation and local anaesthetic injections. That seemed to do the trick eventually.

* * *

I didn't play any cricket for Queensland in December and looked on as New Zealand came and went, splitting a two-Test series 1–1. I played a BBL game with Brisbane Heat the same day as the Sydney Test against India kicked off and felt good, if a little rusty.

Australia held a 2–0 lead in a four-Test series against India heading to Perth and I was called in to the squad. I was part of a four-pronged pace attack with Peter Siddle, Ben Hilfenhaus and Mitch Starc. Pup won the toss and sent India in and it turned out to be a great call. The pitch was doing a bit, and those three boys ripped through the Indian line-up to have them all out for 161 just after tea.

I only managed one wicket, but it was the one that every bowler craved back then: Sachin Tendulkar. When I'm old and grey I'll be able to tell the story of the day I got the little master out at the WACA! I'd bowled a few balls that went away from him a bit, then I got one to go the other way off the pitch and hit him in front. It looked pretty adjacent to me and everyone behind the wicket and the umpire Kumar Dharmasena fired him out, much to our great delight.

We went on to win by an innings and 37 runs to secure the series win. It was good to be back in the fold and I felt like I was moving reasonably well, but I only took one wicket in each innings so I had some work to do heading to Adelaide for the final Test. It would be the tenth Test of my career, my own benchmark for becoming a 'real' Test cricketer, and it was fitting that I reached that mark in my home town.

It was the Ponting–Clarke show over the first two days at Adelaide Oval as Ricky and Pup demoralised India with a double century each. Cricket's a pretty easy game when you're in the dressing-room and you've got two batsmen out in the middle seeing them like beach balls. It was an awesome display and set up a 298-run win to sweep the series.

I took 4 wickets for the Test and was intent on finding more rhythm in the ODI series with Sri Lanka joining India, but I think I actually wanted it too much. I hadn't played an ODI for Australia for over eighteen months by the time we played India in Melbourne. I bowled okay at the MCG without taking a wicket, but then I was expensive and only took one wicket in each of the next three games. I was trying too hard and, as I've said before, when I try to force it is generally when things start to go wrong.

I was dropped after taking 1–43 against Sri Lanka in Hobart and didn't get a look-in for the rest of that series.

I was disappointed with myself after working so hard to get back into the ODI side, but I found a silver lining with Queensland. It was a tight race between the Bulls, Victoria, Tasmania and Western Australia for the two spots in the final that season. It went right down to the wire, but after the last weekend of the season Queensland had won the right to host Tasmania at the Gabba in the 2011–12 Sheffield Shield final.

I'd always loved watching Shield finals on the television as a kid and had always dreamed of playing in one. I'd made a big decision to move to Queensland and it had paid off in terms of my international ambitions, but I was desperate to share in some success with those boys because we were such a tight group.

We were in all sorts at 5–55 in reply to Tassie's first innings of 241, but two really important partnerships between Chris Hartley and James Hopes, then Harts and Steve Magoffin, gave us a 35-run lead.

I was filthy with myself with bowling figures of 0–71 in the first innings, but Alister McDermott was huge for us with a six-for. Hopesy did the damage in their second dig with a five-for and I was at least able to do my bit with 3 wickets as they set us a target of 133 for the win.

It wasn't a big target by any means, but that was one of the most nerve-racking days of cricket in my life. We were moving nicely towards the target at 2–83 when we lost 5 wickets for about 8 runs ... the last of which was me out for a second-ball duck.

Hartley and Magoffin were the heroes again, though, and they saw us home to the absolute delight of the dressing-room. I'd experienced some great moments over the previous two years or so, but that win meant so much to me. I don't mind admitting I teared up a bit when Steve pushed the winning single ... I get emotional just thinking about it years later.

More good news was to come when I was picked for the tour of the West Indies in April. The tour had actually started in March with an ODI in Saint Vincent on the same day the Shield final started. I was still keen to play one-dayers, but I felt like the selectors were keen to try a few different combinations and give a few other guys a go.

There are some stunning spots in the Caribbean and it was another box ticked for me. I always wanted to play the Windies over there and was really keen to play well, but after my disappointment at getting dropped from the ODI team I was equally determined to relax, enjoy it, and just let the game come to me a bit.

That approach paid immediate dividends with the bat in Barbados where I made an unbeaten 68 in our first innings. It was an amazing Test actually: Pup declared while we were still 40-odd runs behind and we skittled them for 148 to chase 192 for the win. It was a tough chase and we lost a few wickets along the way, but the failing light was the big issue. I was in with Hilf at the end with Sidds and Nathan Lyon to come in; but Hilf hit the winning run with the light failing.

I'd been nursing a minor shoulder issue and was rested in the second Test—which was drawn after extensive rain delays—but was back in for the third Test in Dominica. I didn't feel like I bowled terribly, but I only managed one wicket on a real turner. Our skipper even bagged a five-for with his gentle left-armers! We won by 75 runs for a 2–0 series win, which is always a great source of satisfaction when you're away from home.

I went to India for my second stint with Kings XI Punjab following that tour, but my right shoulder was getting progressively worse. I could still bowl okay at the start, but throwing was causing me serious pain. By the end of the series it was starting to hurt when I bowled and I was getting shooting pains when I rolled onto that side when I slept. I was booked in to see a specialist in Melbourne when I got back.

The specialist presented us with two options: the first was to undergo a shoulder reconstruction that would put me out for twelve months, and the second was to have a minor cleanout, which included having a bit of bone scraped away, which would see me still a chance to play some cricket in the Australian summer.

It didn't take me long to choose the second option. I had the operation in August and the plan was that I'd miss the South African tour of Australia in November, but be right by the time Sri Lanka arrived in December. The surgery went well, but the rehabilitation program was long and tedious.

My shoulder injury did have one upside, though: my busy cricket schedule had made it hard for me and Cherie to nail down a wedding date, but with me sidelined for a bit we took the opportunity to get married. She organised our wedding in about three months, which seemed like plenty of time to me, but apparently is quite a short timeframe to put together a wedding!

I'd dealt with plenty of injuries before, but this one really got me down at times. I still wasn't close to bowling by October and I couldn't bring myself to watch the Bulls' first Ryobi Cup match of the season because it made me so frustrated.

I'd been given a range of exercises to help strengthen the joint, which I really smashed into, but my progress was annoyingly slow no matter how much time I put into it. I would work at my program during the day then sit on the couch in front of the television working with a resistance band at night. I couldn't bowl in the nets until the middle of December and I was still getting a lot of pain. Kevin Sims and Adam Smith, physiotherapists with the Australian and Queensland teams respectively, were watching me struggling away in the nets one day and they decided to try a different type of strapping on me.

The main issue I was encountering was that it was very hard to get going when I went to bowl or do weights in the gym because I was so stiff and sore. What Kev and Adam did was strap me from my right armpit to over my left shoulder so that my shoulder blade was positioned differently. I still got a fair bit of soreness, but it allowed me to get going a lot easier. It was a simple thing, so simple that I really didn't think it would make any difference, but that strapping was a major breakthrough in my recovery from that shoulder injury.

The whole episode really drove home to me the need to spend time working with weights to strengthen my back and shoulders. I'd never been a gym rat like Mitch Johnson and had always found lifting weights boring, but that injury gave me a greater appreciation for the role it played in helping get me back out in the middle and staying there.

I steadily improved after Christmas, but it was too late for me to play any part in Australia's 3–0 series win against Sri Lanka or push my case for inclusion in the Test tour of India in March.

My disappointment at being injured and missing the Australian summer was only made worse by the fact I missed the last matches of Ricky Ponting and Mike Hussey. Punter announced his retirement during the South African series and played his last Test in Perth, while Huss called time on his career during the Sri Lankan series and bowed out after the third Test at the SCG. I knew they were both getting towards the end of their careers, but I still thought they had plenty to give, especially with an Ashes tour just around the corner.

Ricky and Mike were a huge part of what made playing for Australia so great for me. Their burning passion for Australian cricket was infectious and I absolutely loved playing cricket with them. I was gutted that I couldn't be there to see them off.

When I was dropped from the Australian one-day side I found getting back and playing for the Bulls immensely satisfying, and it was the same twelve months later after that frustrating summer.

I was cleared to play by the middle of February and was stoked to see Queensland win through to the Ryobi Cup final to be played against Victoria at the MCG.

That was an amazing game to be a part of and will remain one of the highlights of my career. It was an odd game in a lot of respects and one that we looked right out of at times. We were put in by the Vics and lost wickets regularly before we lost about an hour and a half to a rain delay.

The game was reduced to 32 overs each when play resumed and things didn't get better for us at 7–97 with 27 overs gone. Jason Floros really saved the day for us with his innings of 47, including two 6s and a 4 in the last over, getting us to 146.

We were looking all right at 4–42 with James Hopes bagging 2 wickets, but Cameron White and Peter Handscomb steadied things down for them and moved their score along to 105 needing 42 runs from 42 balls. The Vics kept losing wickets, but they only needed 9 runs from the last 2 overs with 3 wickets in hand.

We were right up against it, but Alister McDermott bowled a cracking over. He took a wicket and conceded just 4 runs. One of the big reasons I'd decided to switch to Queensland was that I'd always admired their never-say-die attitude. They only needed 2 runs for the win when Clint McKay and Darren Pattinson singled off my first two deliveries. I held my third ball cross-seamed and wanted to bash the wicket and get the ball through just above the stumps, but it took off on Clint a bit. He tried to fend it down to third man, but edged it to Chris Hartley behind the stumps who took an unbelievable catch over his head. Harts isn't the biggest guy, but he just seemed to keep going up for that catch.

Fawad Ahmed was the last batsman in for the Vics and I didn't know too much about him as a batsman. I had a chat to Hopesy and wondered if I should bounce him, but the skipper decided to put a slip in and told me to put it up to him. I went with the cross seam again and got it down there as quick as I could. Peter Forrest took the catch going to his right. It was a stunning finish to an amazing game.

I took 4 wickets and got Man of the Match, but it really should have gone to Jason Floros: his knock towards the end of our innings was what gave us some hope.

Queensland made it through to another Shield final that year, but we couldn't repeat the success of the season before. Tasmania finished above us on the table and hosted the final at Bellerive, which meant they only needed to draw the match to be awarded the Sheffield Shield.

We were up against it after Tasmania won the toss and made 419 in their first dig. The pitch was lifeless and it was a slog for everyone. Boof wasn't keen for me to bust a boiler but there was a moment on the fourth day when I had a spell that breathed some life into things. I was convinced I had one more big effort in me, and with Tassie 4–6 in their second innings, we were flirting with a miracle. But they weathered that particular Hobart storm and that was our sniff at victory gone. It was shattering when we couldn't get the win, but I was really proud of the way the boys fought it out. I ended up with 145 overs under my belt from three first-class games in twenty days and it was enough for the selectors to keep me safe a few months later when they deliberated over the Ashes squad.

I went to India for another stint with Kings XI not long after the Shield final, but my campaign was short-lived. I developed soreness in my left Achilles tendon, which got progressively worse until I had to pull the pin and go home. I had this big lump on my heel that was very tender, but I saw a specialist who gave me a set of exercises to help.

The other thing I had to do was get my boots modified. The lump on my heel was red raw where my boot made contact with it. They actually cut away a large section from the heel of my boot, which helped a lot.

I needed all the help I could get because after twelve months where it seemed everything that could go wrong did go wrong, I had about twelve weeks to prove I was fit enough to go to England with the Ashes squad.

CHAPTER 19

THE ASHES IN ENGLAND

I had serious doubts over whether I'd be able to get up for the Ashes tour of England in 2013 and I bugged Alex constantly. I'd tell him I was struggling with this or that, he'd tell me I'd be right, which would make me feel a bit better and then we'd repeat the conversation in a few days' time. I'm sure it was very annoying for Alex, but he is blessed with the patience of a saint and happily listened to all my gripes and concerns before giving me a few words of encouragement.

In the back of my mind I knew there had to be some doubt as to whether they'd pick me even if I was fit. Through form and fitness I hadn't put any runs on the board for Australia for over a year, so it was a great relief when I did get the call to say I was in the squad to go to England.

I was included in the Australia A squad, which left before the Ashes side. I was able to get in the bowling I needed, while still rehabbing under the supervision of our strength and conditioning guys. I'll be forever grateful that they did because, even though I didn't play much with Australia A, the early start was what allowed me to take part in that Ashes series.

The ODI squad was in England playing in the ICC Champions Trophy at the same time. The Ashes squad would be made up of players from that squad, the Australia A team, and a few players that were coming out from Australia to join us.

The Australia A team was in Belfast preparing to take on Ireland in a four-day game when we heard about Dave Warner's unfortunate dust-up with Joe Root in a Birmingham bar.

It was disappointing and Davey knew he'd let himself and the team down. It was an unwanted distraction over a bit of mucking around in a pub, but that's all it takes sometimes. It wasn't like he knocked him out or anything close to that, but Davey certainly paid a big price. We paid a price too because there's no doubt our team is better with him in it.

In a strange way it might have been the making of Dave Warner as a cricketer, though. It was a harsh lesson, but one he'll probably tell you himself he needed to learn.

There was even more drama in store for us, though.

We were in Bristol for the last game of the Australia A tour, where Darren Lehmann was the assistant coach. Towards the end of the game, Boof went missing, which was a bit odd. Peter Siddle came up to me and he reckoned something was going on. Boof was always there on the sideline offering advice and encouraging words when we were out on the park. But he was nowhere to be seen for a few hours there.

He showed up again around the time we finished and he was being very coy. I asked where he'd been, but he just said that he had a few things to take care of.

Of course, Mickey Arthur was sacked that day and Boof was brought in to replace him as coach of the national team. Boof was sworn to secrecy until Cricket Australia made all the proper arrangements. CA's chief executive, James Sutherland, and general manager of team performance, Pat Howard, were over and they would be the ones to inform everyone and then make the move public.

I was shocked when I found out—we all were. Mickey had been in charge since Tim Nielsen resigned late in 2011. Unfortunately, I was injured for a fair bit of that period and I'd only played a handful of games under him. He's a great bloke and you don't like to see anyone lose their job, but CA clearly felt the need to go in another direction and they acted.

I went with a few of the boys to visit Mickey in his room and it was quite emotional. We all wanted to thank him for what he'd done for us and wish him all the best, but he was clearly devastated and I felt like our words didn't mean much at the time.

The timing of it, so close to the start of an Ashes campaign, clearly wasn't ideal, but any misgivings I had were put to rest when I was told Darren Lehmann would be taking over. To have someone I really respected and had such a long history with in charge of the Australian team would not only be good for me, but also for the whole team: I knew how good a coach he was. He'd done a great job with Queensland and the boys were all really impressed with what he'd been able to do in the few short weeks on the Australia A tour. He was a popular choice.

The rest of the Ashes squad was coming up to join us in Bristol the next day and Michael Clarke sat in the press conference where Boof was announced as our new coach. The press were all over it because it was obviously a huge story, but we had to try to put that behind us as quickly as we could.

It was good to hook up with the rest of the Ashes squad and we kept moving on to Somerset, where we were due to play our first tour match. Here we had our first official meeting with the new coach.

Boof presented a vision that wasn't too dissimilar to the one he gave us when he took over at Queensland. He wasn't going to change who he was or what he believed in depending on the circumstances. He was taking over the biggest job in Australian cricket at a critical time, but he still stood up there and said, 'This is me, this is what I'm about and this is what I expect of you.' It was a simple but effective message.

He put up a Cricket Australia slide of a list of trademarks or behaviours that we had put together as a team. Nothing groundbreaking, most elite sports teams do the same thing. Stuff like, 'I will leave no stone unturned in my preparation ...' But he grabbed a texta and drew a big line across the whole list. His point was that every sentence started with the word

'I' and that under his guidance there would be no 'I' any more—it was 'we' from that point on.

We finished the meeting and went straight to the pub. Everyone had a beer and we just got on with it.

Boof felt really bad for Mickey—we all did—but we had a job to do and that was to move forward and win the Ashes. He adjusted to the role so smoothly that it quickly seemed like he'd been in charge for ages.

I played against Worcestershire in our last warm-up game before the first Test. I knew my form wasn't quite there even before Boof came and told me he didn't think I would be right to go when the series kicked off at Trent Bridge.

I got a couple of wickets in each innings, but my pace wasn't where it needed to be. My Achilles and knee issues meant that I hadn't bowled enough to find my rhythm. I was disappointed to hear that, but I knew he was right.

It was tough watching the boys start the series from the dressing-room, but I continued to increase my workload in the nets the first two days of the Test and then had a breakthrough on day three.

I'd been a bit worried about a few different parts of my action and how my body was holding up, but I decided to go out and really put it all on the line, which was an approach that had worked for me in the past. I went out to the practice pitch, which was actually out on the ground, with Ali de Winter, our bowling coach, during the lunch break and had a session that really set up my whole Ashes campaign. Something just seemed to click and I felt like I'd found the rhythm that had eluded me so far on the tour. My Achilles felt good, my knee was okay and they were coming out of my hand better than they had in months: I was ready to go.

That first Test was a tough one to watch, though. We played well in patches with some excellent individual performances, like Peter Siddle's five-for in the first innings and Ashton Agar's brilliant 98 on debut. But we couldn't get over the line.

It was great to see Ash come in and do what he did. He hadn't even been spoken of in terms of playing Test cricket in the weeks leading up to the series, but the way that he handled himself after being given that opportunity was really impressive. His innings certainly gave us a sniff after we were in huge trouble at 9–117 in reply to England's first innings of 215.

Stuart Broad's refusal to walk after nicking one to Michael Clarke at first slip when England was 6–297 was a massive talking point. We were angry about it at the time, but he doesn't have to walk if he doesn't want to—those are the rules. It didn't look great and I'd like to think I would walk in the same situation, but he was well within his rights to stand his ground if the umpire doesn't do his job and give him out.

With 311 to chase for the win, the boys did a great job on a tricky fifth-day wicket, but fell 14 runs short. We were shattered that we lost that game, but we felt that we'd taken some positive steps and it was great to see Ash get his career off on the right foot.

It seems strange to say it but, even though we lost, the group felt really strong. We'd been through a bit already, it felt like we were under siege a bit when the Dave Warner/ Mickey Arthur stuff happened, so to come out and play like that for the new coach really seemed to bring everyone closer.

I was walking across the hallowed turf at Lord's when I found out I had been picked for the second Test.

We'd just finished our main training session and I was on my way back to the dressing-room when I saw Boof walking towards me with Rod Marsh, who had been on the National Selection Panel since late 2011.

Boof told me not to react to what he was about to say, because there were a few media types with cameras around the place. When he told me I was in the side to play in the second Test, I broke out into a huge smile and immediately got told off by Boof because they always try to keep team selection news under wraps for as long as they can.

I thought our bowlers had done a decent job in the first Test and I didn't think I was a shot to get back in, so it was a great surprise. It had been over a year since I'd played my last Test against the West Indies over in the Caribbean. To be able to shake off my injury concerns and fulfil a long-held dream to play a Test match at the home of cricket was more than I could have hoped for.

My last experience of Lord's, when I'd suffered a reoccurrence of my knee injury in the one-dayer against England in 2010, had been a disappointing one. I was determined to have a better time of it this time around.

Lord's is such a magical ground—the Father Time weather-vane, the Long Room, the pavilion, the honour boards, the slope of the ground—it all combines to make playing cricket there something special. Even the lunches are the best in world cricket!

Another part of what makes a Lord's Test match so great is that you get to meet Her Majesty the Queen. It was quite a surreal feeling to be out on the ground on the first day of play, but then to suddenly have the Queen standing in front of me was something I'll never forget.

She actually stopped in front of me as she came down the line of players and said something about bringing the nice weather with us. I don't remember what I said because my mind was reeling. She's only a small lady, but she's a massive figure on the world scene, and it was a real honour to meet her. I could just imagine what my dad and grandparent's would have made of that, as former subjects.

I opened the bowling with James Pattinson. Patto came on at the Nursery end and I came from the Pavilion end. Bowling at Lord's is a little different to most other grounds because of the famous slope of the wicket.

I didn't really have a preference as to which end I bowled from, but I know a lot of bowlers have strong feelings about where they operate from at Lord's because they feel the slope is a big factor. Standing at the top of your mark from the Pavilion end, the left edge of the pitch is higher than the right edge, which is why it's referred to as bowling 'down the slope' when you come in from that end. Apparently the northern end of the ground is about 2.5 metres higher than the southern end, which is quite amazing.

The theory is that it's quite difficult to swing the ball away from right-handed batsmen when you're bowling down the slope at them, but I was reasonably happy with the movement I was able to get both ways.

Glenn McGrath was spending a bit of time with the team at the time and it was really helpful to be able to pick his brain because he bowled almost exclusively from the Pavilion end during his career—with great success.

We got off to a good start that morning with Shane Watson striking first to dismiss Alastair Cook before I managed to trap Joe Root in front and then get Kevin Pietersen edging to Brad Haddin. We had to have them 3–28.

England really dug in, though, and we were disappointed when they were 7–289 at stumps and went on to score 361. I'd looked at the honour boards in the grand old pavilion with great envy, so to be able to take a five-for in that innings and get my own name up there was really humbling.

Jimmy Anderson edged one to Hadds for my five-for. Holding that ball up to the crowd at that storied ground will always be a special moment for me. Unfortunately, things started to get away from us as the Test progressed. We didn't bat well and we were all out for 128 before England went back in and took the match away from us with 7–349 in their second innings.

Set a target of 583, we were all out for 235. To lose by 347 runs is a disappointing loss in anyone's language. To get so close in the first Test and then serve up something like that in the second was a huge disappointment for all of us. I could tell Boof was angry, but he has a good way of getting his point across without flying off the handle. He didn't need to say much, to be honest, because we all knew the areas we hadn't performed well in. We would have to work hard before the third Test at Old Trafford.

Being on a long tour like the Ashes can be quite mentally draining, but Boof and his management team made sure we had opportunities to spend a bit of down time with our partners and families.

Most of the guys who played at Lord's were excused from the tour match against Sussex before the third Test and I stayed back in London with Shane Watson, Peter Siddle and Chris Rogers. Cherie had flown out to join me just before the first Test and it was just as well she had because I would probably have spent most of those rest days in bed if she wasn't there.

I was very sore after my first Test in over a year, but Cherie wasn't having any of my complaining. We stayed at a great hotel called the Royal Garden, just near Kensington Palace and Hyde Park. It's a brilliant part of the city and Cherie got me up and outside walking around. I love London as a city and the weather was fantastic, so I enjoyed having a look around and it helped me work out a few sore spots as well.

Gav had flown over with his family as well so it was great to be able to spend a bit of time with them too.

We hired a car and drove the two hours down to Hove on the south coast to watch a bit of the tour match against Sussex and then we drove ourselves up to Manchester. It was a good five-hour trip and it was great to be able to spend some time with Cherie and see a few of the sights.

We got some bad news ahead of the third Test: James Pattinson was sent home with stress fractures in his lower back. I'd gotten to know James quite well and I was shattered for him given the amount of work he'd done to get himself fit again. You never like to lose a teammate from a tour; I'd been in his position before and knew how he was feeling. We were all disappointed for him.

Preparing properly for a Test match is always important, but possibly even more so when you're on a long tour. There was a fair bit of science behind a bowler's preparation by the time I arrived on the Australian scene. The conditioning guys made sure you were ready to go at just the right time.

Basically, I'd work backwards from standing at the top of my mark to bowl my first ball of a Test. It's all about making sure you've got just the right bowling load into you when you arrive at that point, and that varies between different bowlers.

Two days out from a Test is the big training day for us. I generally like to get out and have a good bowl, which is normally about 6 to 8 overs in the nets. Then I have a bat and a decent workout.

If that day goes to plan and I'm feeling good then the day before a Test will generally be a bit of a catching session, something light. Or if Alex or I don't feel like I've got enough done the day before then I'll bowl another over or two to top up my preparation.

Each time we bowl in the nets we make a note of how many balls we've bowled that session. It all goes into a graph that plots our progress. A week out, our conditioning guys might say that I need to have 180 balls under my belt by the time I get to two days out from a Test.

It's quite a juggling act to get yourself at the right level. You don't want to be too fatigued, but you want to feel like you've got your eye in.

I always wake up with good nerves and excitement the morning of a Test match. Generally, that's pretty early and I'll get downstairs and have some breakfast, although I don't generally eat much before a day's play. There's usually an early bus to the ground and then a slightly later one that most of the guys will be on. I like to be on that main bus on the first day of a Test because I like to arrive at the ground as a team.

I don't have any superstitions or rituals with my preparation on match day, but the main thing is I don't like to feel rushed. Like most things in life, if I feel like I've done everything I can then that gives me the base of confidence I need to perform.

We were determined to hit back hard after a poor showing at Lord's, and we did, but England still retained the Ashes at Old Trafford.

We batted very well, the bowlers did their bit and I'm certain we would have won that Test match if we'd had a decent run with the weather. You're not going to lose too many matches if you declare for 527 in your first innings.

Pup made a brilliant 187 with Chris Rogers, Steve Smith, Brad Haddin and Mitch Starc making half-centuries, and it was pretty obvious early on that England was content to play for the draw. Sidds was our best bowler with four-for as we bowled them out for 368, which they made at a pedestrian 2.63 runs an over. I got a couple of wickets, Trott and Bell, but I wasn't happy with my line on a few occasions.

We lost wickets regularly as we went looking for quick runs with the weather forecast looking grim. The umpires called play off early on day four due to bad light. I was out in the middle with the skipper when they did and he was unimpressed to say the least. We were fine to continue on, but the umpires had asked Alastair Cook if he wanted to bring on his spinners because a few of their fielders were complaining it was difficult to pick up the ball. Of course, he said he'd rather not and the umpires took us off. It robbed us of valuable overs at the English batsmen in the evening session.

Dave Warner had been welcomed back into the team for that Test and he top-scored in the second innings with 41 before he was caught in the deep by none other than Joe Root. At least Davey could see the funny side of the whole affair by then—'Hooked another one at Rooty', he said with a wry grin when he did media at the end of that day. He's a top bloke, Davey, and I was impressed with the way he fought back after being sent off to South Africa. He was the villain as far as English fans were concerned for the rest of the summer. A trumpeter played the 'Rocky' movie theme when he went out to bat, which was actually pretty funny, and he got booed relentlessly, but he seemed to take it all in his stride.

Michael declared overnight with a 332-run lead, but the weather took a turn for the worse on the last day.

We started late due to persistent rain, but when we did get at them we got off to just the start we were after. The wicket was doing a bit and I managed to get one to come back in on Cook. We were ecstatic when Tony Hill gave him out, but had to wait for a DRS call, which came back in our favour anyway. I was really confident we could bowl them out and I felt like I was bowling as well as I had for a while.

I was sure I had Trott out LBW a few overs later, but umpire Hill wasn't interested in our appeals. Pup sent it to review and even though it showed the ball clipping the stumps it stayed with the umpire's call on the ground—much to my frustration! Trott edged one to Hadds soon after that, so there was some satisfaction there, but the inconsistency of the DRS was an issue throughout the series.

When Sidds dismissed Kevin Pietersen caught behind we were looking good at 3–27. That's when it started to go pear-shaped. We only got 3 more overs at them before lunch and a shower delayed the resumption of play by about twenty minutes. Sidds bowled 3 balls to Ian Bell and then the heavens opened. I hate rain delays, but I've never felt angrier at the weather than I was that day. What should have been a fighting win to claw back to 2–1 in the series ended in England retaining the Ashes when the umpires abandoned play and the match ended in a draw.

It was a quick turnaround between the third and fourth Tests, so we had to shake off our disappointment quickly. The Ashes might have been gone, but we were determined to win one or both of the remaining Tests and take some momentum into the Australian Ashes series, which would get underway less than three months after the fifth Test at The Oval finished.

There was a bit of history about the fourth Test because it was to be played at the Riverside Ground in Chester-le-

Street, which is Durham's home ground, and it would be the first time an Ashes Test had been played there. The Riverside is only a small ground, but it has a nice country feel to it. It's up in the north-east of England, just south of Newcastle. I'd never been up that far before, so it was good to have a look around. Not that we got too much time for sightseeing.

The wicket was pretty flat and dry—nearly all of them were that summer—but Nathan Lyon managed to coax a bit out of it and bagged 4 wickets. England was all out for 238 early on the second day after winning the toss and having a bat. Chris Rogers made an excellent ton in our first dig, but apart from Watto, who made 68, no-one really stayed with him as we put up a total of 270.

Everyone was really chuffed to see Chris hit his maiden Test century. He'd batted well without luck most of the series and it was a fitting reward for his persistence.

I've spoken before about feeling 'in the zone' and they were certainly coming out nicely in the England second innings. I wish I could replicate the ball that clipped Joe Root's off-stump whenever I wanted to, but they're all too rare. It was just full enough to bring him forward, but then it went away from him and sent the bails flying.

I was really happy with my pace and control and managed to snare Cook and Trott, but Bell and KP came together and put on a good partnership for England. They advanced the score to 155 after we'd had them 3–49, before Lyon removed KP on 44.

They were 5–234 going into the fourth day, but their tail wagged a little more than we would've liked. The wickets kept coming for me, but they'd made it to 330, leaving us a target of 299 runs before we bowled them out. I finished with career-best figures of 7–117, but I don't get much satisfaction from those figures given the way the match ended. I would have gladly gone without a wicket if we could've chased down those runs. It wasn't to be.

Once again, we were left frustrated after we worked our way into a strong position only to fail to push home our advantage. Chris Rogers and Dave Warner put on a 109-run partnership to open our run chase, but Stuart Broad bowled a superb spell to finish with 6–50. We collapsed to be all out for 224 with England winning by 74 runs and taking a 3–0 series lead.

'Gutted' doesn't come close to describing how we felt. Boof wasn't happy with how we batted and fair enough too, but he was right onto us about getting back up for the fifth Test. We had a team dinner, as we do after every Test, and I received the gold blazer, which was something Boof had brought in to acknowledge the team's best player of the match. They get it embroidered with your name, your figures and the Test match details and you wear it that night until you have to give it back for the next Test. It was a good bit of fun and a nice way to acknowledge good performances from the boys, but I didn't feel much like wearing it that night. The team was so close on that tour and we enjoyed spending time together, but everyone was hurting a bit that night.

Most of the team travelled to Northampton to play an England Lions side over three days in the gap between the fourth and fifth Tests, but I went back down to London with

Brad Haddin and Peter Siddle. We were all a bit sore and needed the rest. My knee was playing up a bit, but there was no way I was going to miss the last Test.

James Faulkner was brought in to make his debut and it was great to see him get some reward for effort. Shane Warne presented him with his baggy green on the ground, which is always a special moment.

The Oval is another one of England's most historic grounds and it was good to be finishing the series there. We were pumped to finish strong and Shane Watson and Steve Smith certainly batted that way after the skipper won the toss. Watto made a brilliant 176, while Steve batted well with 138 not out.

Pup declared at 9–492 with about 20 overs left on the second day after it had rained for most of the first half of the day. It was a good wicket to bat on and most of the England batsmen got a start, but none went on to make a hundred as we bowled them out for 377. But that didn't happen until the fifth day! We lost the entire fourth day of play due to persistent rain, which was frustrating to say the least. James Faulkner was the best of our bowlers, taking 4 wickets, which was great to see from a young fella in his first Test.

The skipper was intent on getting a result—we all were—despite the limited time available. After a spirited session with the bat we set them a target of 227 to get from 44 overs after tea.

I opened the bowling with Starcy and managed to get Joe Root caught behind. It was Brad Haddin's twenty-ninth catch of the series, which broke Rod Marsh's record that had stood for thirty years. We celebrate each other's achievements in the Australian team and we were all thrilled for Hadds, who was a rock for us behind the stumps the whole series.

Still, England looked to be gaining the upper hand with Cook and Trott advancing their score to 86 before Faulkner trapped Cook in front. We just couldn't spark the batting collapse we needed, though. They were 3–163 when Davey Warner took a good outfield catch off my bowling to dismiss Pietersen, but that would be my last over of the series.

I'd been receiving some treatment for a sore hamstring and, as much as I hated to, I had to go off to get Alex to work on it some more with 9 overs remaining in the game. The floodlights were on and it was very dark by then. We managed another 2 wickets—Ian Bell's run-out was our first of the series—with Bell's dismissal coming from the last ball before the umpires abandoned play due to poor light. England still needed 21 runs from 4 overs to win.

Michael Clarke had done his best to set up a result, but we were booed by the England crowd as the players walked off, which I thought was a bit rich.

We went and shook hands with the England boys and looked on as the presentations were made, which was pretty gut-wrenching to be honest. We'd fought hard and I felt we deserved better than a 3–0 result, but there's no denying England was the better team across the series. We let ourselves down with a bad session here and there and good teams will make you pay for that—which England did.

The mood was subdued in our rooms before we went over to the England rooms to have a beer with them. It had been a hard-fought series, which did get a little edgy at times. But you'd expect nothing less when two teams are hell-bent on winning the same prize.

We stayed and had a drink with them for an hour or so, then we were off back to our hotel. We had our customary dinner and a few drinks and it was good to be able to let go of a bit of the pressure that had been building. There was plenty of disappointment, but also some relief and, actually, a fair bit of optimism as well.

No-one gave us a chance when we went over there, but we did ourselves proud with some of our efforts. With a bit of luck the result could have been different and we were already looking towards the return series in Australia.

CHAPTER 20

RETURN THE URN

I was cooked by the time I got home from England ... physically and mentally fried. I'd never been on a more demanding tour, but despite the toll it took I loved every minute of it. We had failed to win the Ashes, but England would be on our home soil in less than three months and I couldn't wait— we were going to throw absolutely everything we had at them.

We did a lot of planning for our approach to that series and one of the main things we wanted to do was make them uncomfortable with the bat and the ball. As a bowling group we were going to be aggressive. And who better to add some venom to our mix than Mitch Johnson?

Mitch hadn't played a Test since March that year and he'd gone away and worked his butt off to get back into the side. He'd become a father as well, and he seemed to have a different perspective on cricket when he got back into the side. He cared so much about playing for his country, sometimes it seemed he was carrying the weight of the world on his shoulders. I think being a dad helped him relax about his cricket a bit.

I knew he'd come back bigger and better and he played his way back into the Test side with some strong performances in the one-day team in England and India. I got a text from Brad Haddin from India and he reckoned he'd never seen Mitch bowl as fast as he was over there. He can bowl quicker than me off four steps, so to have him, fit, firing and in form in our side would be a huge bonus.

We knew we'd made some inroads with some of their batsmen in England and we were keen to turn up the heat on our own turf. They'd been very successful in Australia in the 2010–11 series and, worse than that, they'd enjoyed playing here. We were determined to give them as hostile a reception as we possibly could.

I was feeling good going into the series. I'd played four Tests in a row in England and I was confident with the management plan we had in place that I could play through the whole series at home. I was seeing David Young regularly, with one of the key treatments getting injections of platelet-rich plasma into the joint. Platelet-rich plasma is meant to help with the cushioning in the joint and even encourage some cartilage growth. I hate needles—I don't know anyone who likes them—but I *really* hate needles and my knee issues meant that I had to have lots of them.

But I was confident with where we were at with the knee and Boof said that if I put my hand up and I was bowling well then he'd pick me for five Tests, which gave me a lot of confidence.

We felt like we were prepared up to the minute as the first Test started at the Gabba. The planning was done, the bowlers had the right amount of overs into them and the batsmen had worked hard in the nets. There's nothing quite like the nervous tension and excitement the morning a new series starts. With so much on the line I couldn't wait to get hostilities underway.

Pup won the toss and had a bat, which was a good way to start things off. We got the hostility we were after in Stuart Broad's first over. He was loudly booed by the crowd, but even better, Davey Warner dispatched his first ball to the boundary with a cracking pull shot. It was just the sort of tone-setting aggression we were after, but we didn't follow it up as well as we would have liked with the bat.

Broad was always going to be the villain after his decision not to walk back in England, but he took the boos in his stride and bowled very well, taking 6 wickets in our first innings.

Hadds top-scored for us with 94 and Mitch Johnson was next with 64. Similar to the Perth Test three years earlier when he made a half-century, he backed up his good work on the bat with the ball.

We would have liked to have scored more than 295, but we also knew that the pitch was nowhere near as flat as it was back in 2010–11 when the first Test ended in a draw with over 1300 runs scored. We planned to keep testing Alastair Cook down that fourth or fifth stump line and

I got him fishing outside off-stump in my sixth over. Then Mitch removed Jonathan Trott with a short ball just before lunch. George Bailey took a ripping catch at mid-wicket off my bowling to have them struggling at 3–82. It was just what we'd talked about in our planning: 'Don't let them get comfortable.'

We took it up a notch just before tea when Mitch took 3 wickets. Nathan Lyon was on a hat-trick as England lost 5 wickets for 4 runs to be in all sorts at 8–91. Mitch was bowling the sort of intimidating spell that makes the opposition sit up and take notice … and also sows the seed of doubt in the batsman's mind, which makes it easier for the rest of us.

England was all out for 136, and Dave Warner and Michael Clarke set about putting the game beyond their reach. Both made brilliant hundreds and we set up a big lead with Pup declaring 561 runs in front with about an hour left on day three.

They're always tricky sessions for batsmen and we got the result that we were after when Mitch and I got rid of Jonathan Trott and Michael Carberry respectively.

There was a lot made of the way Trott got out. We'd been working him over with the short ball for a while and when he took the bait again Dave Warner tried to get under his skin a bit by describing it as 'pretty poor and weak' in his press conference after the day's play.

They were pretty direct words from Davey and they looked terrible when Trott made his shock announcement that he was going home due to a stress-related illness. Davey didn't know that at the time he made those comments, of course, and he apologised for them later. I felt for Trott because mental illness is obviously a very serious matter.

Dave was probably allowing his on-field manner to spill over into the press room a bit there. I'm sure opposition teams would consider him very annoying on the field because he's always got something to say, but that's part of getting under a batsman's skin. He just sits at backward point and chirps away all day. He's a real terrier out on the field and we love that about him.

England were staring down the barrel, but they put up some stiff resistance early on day four before Mitch struck again to finish the innings with a five-for and a well-deserved Man of the Match award.

He caught Jimmy Anderson off his own bowling to finish the Test and get our series off to a brilliant start.

* * *

It was a shame that a bit of the gloss got taken off that by the controversy around Michael Clarke's sledge when he told Jimmy to 'get ready for a broken f***ing arm'. A lot was made of it, and it certainly didn't sound nice in isolation, but I think the most disappointing thing was that it went to air in the first place. Channel Nine does a brilliant job with the broadcast of our great game, but that was an unfortunate slip. We're out there in the heat of the battle and things get said—on both sides—but that's just part of the game and has been for as long as I can remember. They were harsh words meant to intimidate, but Jimmy is a big boy—as well as a world-class sledger in his own right—and he didn't take a backward step.

They'd had us under the pump over the past three series and hadn't been shy in letting us know about it, but things were different now and we wanted to ram that point home in no uncertain terms.

We took a lot of confidence out of that performance and were determined to keep the ball rolling in Adelaide. Michael Clarke won the toss again and we had a bat on an Adelaide Oval that looked a fair bit different to the one I'd grown up playing on.

The SACA's multimillion-dollar makeover of the stadium was almost done and I loved what they were able to achieve. The new grandstand didn't look out of place and I was so happy that they kept a section of the old hill and, of course, the famous old scoreboard. I think it's a great blend of the old and the new.

The wicket hadn't changed all that much, though, and it was still a good one for batsmen. Pup and Hadds took full advantage with a century each as we batted into the evening session on the second day. It was important to get a big score on the board, of course, but it also achieved another goal in wearing down their bowlers a bit. We hadn't made them bowl many overs over the past two Ashes series and even if we weren't scoring at a decent clip all the time, it was important to keep them out there toiling away in the hot Aussie sun.

I certainly appreciated spending a bit of time out in the middle with the bat. And I got to see what all the fuss was about for these batsmen when I got to raise my bat having scored a half-century in a big first innings total of 570.

Mitch Johnson blasted Alastair Cook out in an awkward little session before stumps and carried on his good work the next day. Nathan Lyon and Peter Siddle got rid of Joe Root and KP next morning before Ian Bell and Michael Carberry put together a decent partnership.

Then Mitch stepped up with another fierce spell of bowling. He got rid of Stokes, Prior and Broad with the score on 117—you could see all three of Stuart Broad's stumps, he'd moved so far across to the offside and Mitch didn't miss. He was on a hat-trick twice in that innings and it would have been great if he could have got one, but he was pretty happy with a seven-for. His big dirty handlebar mo' was in full flight by then and so was he!

Jimmy Anderson had been a thorn in our side for too long and I think the way Mitch smashed his middle stump out of the ground and sent him on his way was a reflection off the shift in momentum.

They were 398 runs behind when we went back in and put on a quick 132. Davey Warner put on another solid half-century before Pup declared and set them a target of 531 in the last two days. Mitch got Cook hooking in his first over of the fourth day. I would have loved to have seen him go on and get 10 for the match, but that was his only wicket in the Poms' second dig.

Joe Root and Kevin Pietersen put up some solid resistance to take the game into the fifth day before Peter Siddle was brought on to remove KP, as he had a habit of doing. Sidds struck early on day five to get rid of Broad and I earned my keep with a couple of wickets including the last one of the Test—always a nice feeling when you've won by 218 runs. Up on the big screen on the hill were the words 'Australia leads series 2–0'. I remember thinking what a beautiful sight that was.

* * *

England hadn't won a Test match in Perth for over thirty years and we weren't about to let them break that drought. We didn't need any extra motivation, but it was Michael Clarke's hundredth Test and you always want to do well for someone in a big milestone like that. He acknowledged it in the lead-in, but he certainly made it clear that personal milestones weren't what we were in Perth for. He made sure our focus stayed on achieving our team goals.

Pup did the right thing and won the toss again. He chose to have a bat, but the first day didn't exactly go to plan. We weren't looking great at 5–143, but Steve Smith stepped up and made a crucial ton. He'd scored his maiden Test century at The Oval at the back end of the last series and I was really happy for him, personally, that he was able to follow it up in Perth. I was also delighted from a team point of view because we needed the runs!

Still, to be all out for 385 on the second morning of a Test isn't a shocking position to be in, and we were keen to get out there and have a good crack at the England openers. Cook and Carberry frustrated us, though, as they pushed the score along to 0–85. I decided to change things up a bit and went around the wicket to Carberry. I got just the little piece of luck you need. He tried to leave my first delivery coming from a different angle, but the ball caught the toe of his bat and cannoned back onto his stumps.

Two great catches by Warner and Johnson were huge for us in the evening session. Davey took a good diving catch at point to get rid of Cook, who had looked reasonably comfortable until then, and Mitch's effort throwing himself backwards removed Kevin Pietersen. Peter Siddle was bowling, of course, which made it the tenth time Sidds had dismissed KP in Test cricket.

England resumed at 4–180 on the third day and I managed to get one to come back in and hit Ian Bell on the pads in the third over of the session. We all went up, but umpire Erasmus didn't like the look of it. I thought it was a good shout and the skipper agreed, so he sent it upstairs and the DRS came back in our favour to give us just the start we were after. Ian Bell had been a rock for England in the middle order with three centuries in the previous series and we always liked to see the back of him.

When Mitch got Ben Stokes caught behind a few overs later we were into the tail and bowled them out for 251 before lunch. We'd started a little hesitantly in our first innings, but Chris Rogers and Dave Warner batted beautifully on their way to a 157-run opening partnership before Buck Rogers was out to a great catch by Carberry at point.

Davey motored on to his second ton of the series and it was bloody impressive to watch. There are few batsmen in the world who match him for pure power and he certainly hit them out of the middle that day as he helped move us into a winning position. Not to be outdone, Shane Watson clubbed five 6s in his first century since his 176 back at The Oval. Watto and George Bailey were both key figures as we looked for quick runs—each hit three 6s in single overs from Graeme Swann and Jimmy Anderson respectively.

We'd spoken a lot coming into the series about Jimmy being one of the leaders of their attack. Our batsmen worked hard to lessen his impact. He only had 7 wickets by the end of the third Test and had been expensive, so I think that was mission accomplished.

Pup declared 504 in front just before lunch on the fourth day and it was all there in front of us—the batsmen had done their bit and if the bowlers could hold up their end of the bargain the Ashes would be ours again.

We knew England would click as a batting group at some stage and even though the WACA had been a graveyard for them for decades, we weren't taking anything for granted.

So it was a pretty good time to bowl what I consider to be the best ball of my life in any form of the game. Pup flicked me the cherry to open the bowling and I tried to get it down to Alastair Cook on a good line and length—much the same way that I do every time I open the bowling—but the planets aligned for me. The ball felt good coming out of my hand, it held its line and maybe even came in a bit before it landed on a good length and left him just enough to clip the off bail.

I went nuts and ran straight through all my teammates jumping up and down and trying to throw high-fives, but mostly missing. Being so early in the session, everyone except for George Bailey, who had a helmet on because he was fielding in close, was wearing their baggy greens. To remember us all huddled in that sea of green makes me proud years later. It was a career ball ... in terms of what it did and the timing of it. I don't think I've bowled a better one. I've spent years trying to bowl something like that ball and for it to happen at that stage was unbelievable.

It actually hit the bail so flush that it broke. I made sure I grabbed the bail and it now has a special place in my home and always will.

We were hoping that might spark a bit of a collapse but, to their credit, the England batsmen really made us earn it. We had a couple of reviews go our way, but Bell and Stokes batted well until Bell nicked one behind where Hadds took the catch. They were 5–249 at stumps on day four and we were disappointed with how we bowled.

Boof had a crack at the bowlers when we got back into the dressing-room and it was fair enough too. We'd been too keen to wrap it up and had been too attacking. We strayed from the plans we had in place, which removed some of the pressure on the England batsmen that we'd worked so hard to build.

I've never really struggled with anxiety or nerves that would keep me awake before matches, but I hardly slept a wink that night. I lay in bed thinking about the day's play and how poorly we'd bowled after a good start. I wanted to redeem myself after that finish and I thought a lot about how I was going to go about that the next day. I wanted that urn so badly—we all did—and it could be snatched away just like that. Stranger things have happened in cricket.

I was up early getting treatment in the team room. Everyone was up and about earlier than normal on that final day. There was a tension in the air that I could almost touch. We wanted to get back on the field and get the job done and it seemed to take ages for that first ball to be bowled.

That tension only built as Matt Prior and Ben Stokes batted very well through the first 18 overs of the day, despite the cracks in the pitch really starting to open up. Mitch broke through with the wicket of Prior, but then Tim Bresnan stuck around with Stokes until lunch.

Stokes batted very well for his maiden Test century, which was also England's first for the series, so it was a key moment when Nathan Lyon coaxed an edge that Hadds took very well in the third over after lunch. It wasn't much of a relief, though. I reckon I had my heart in my mouth until Mitch Johnson (who else?) got Jimmy Anderson to pop one up to George Bailey at short leg to seal the win.

I was down at fine leg at the time and I didn't know what had happened until I saw all the guys going nuts. I ran in and jumped into the huddle for what was just a sheer outpouring of joy and pent-up tension. It was the most amazing feeling because we'd worked so hard for no result in England. To stick at it, keep working, and turn it around made it so satisfying for the group.

I always loved sitting in the rooms with the boys after a win and that was a special time for all of us. I sat down with Mitch, Sidds and Nathan for a bit and we were all as cooked as each other. I needed a couple of beers just to start to feel human again and there was more than a bit of the sponsor's product sprayed around the room.

Shane Warne had organised a function for us through his connections with Crown Casino, so we migrated there after an hour or so at the ground. It was a great night with all the support staff and some Aussie cricket greats popping in—but the main thing was that we were all there together. We'd climbed the mountain together and to be able to share that feeling with those guys was something I'll always cherish.

I flew to Melbourne a little worse for wear the next morning to go and have my knee checked out by David Young. Unfortunately, I had to make a quick stop in front of some reporters and television cameras so I could apologise for a regrettable tweet I'd sent out late in proceedings the night before.

We'd had a great evening at a superb show put on by Warnie and Crown, but when we went to move to a different part of the complex we weren't allowed in at first by security staff. I took the opportunity to vent my frustrations on Twitter with a foul-mouthed tweet that wasn't befitting an Australian Test cricketer. It also showed a distinct lack of gratitude towards Crown for putting on a great turn for us.

I learned a valuable lesson about alcohol and social media and I tried my best to apologise the next day despite having just about lost my voice. We'd just accomplished something remarkable and the last thing I wanted to do was take the focus away from that.

* * *

We had claimed the series win 3–0, but there were no dead rubbers as far as we were concerned. England was struggling and we were intent on pressing home the advantage: we wanted 5–0 now.

The Poms lost a player from the Perth team with Graeme Swann retiring suddenly, which we didn't quite know what to make of.

It seemed a bit like things hadn't gone England's way, so he took his bat and his ball and went home. He said he was injured and you have to take him at his word, but to just up and pull the plug on your teammates in the middle of a series didn't seem the right way to go. Whatever his reasons, it certainly gave us plenty of motivation to keep going hard at England.

Boxing Day is a huge day on the Australian cricket calendar and we wanted to make sure we kept our momentum going. It was a bit of a case of unfinished business for me as well. I limped off the MCG with a broken ankle the last time I played a Test there and I wanted to create a few happier memories.

I got to do that straight away when Michael Clarke won the toss and decided to put England in. I'd watched Boxing Day Tests since I was a boy and that moment when the bowler stands at the top of his mark to bowl the first ball of an epic five-day contest was always massive for me. I dreamed of doing it myself and I was over the moon when Pup threw me the ball.

The MCG was packed that first morning. Just over 91,000 people—a new record—were at the ground and bowling that first ball was something I'll always remember. I don't often remember specific moments when I'm standing at the top of my mark, but that one will live with me forever.

England batted well, if very slowly, on a pitch that looked a bit green. Pup had put them in thinking it might do a bit more, but they toiled away and would have been reasonably happy to be 6–226 at stumps on day one. We cleaned them up pretty quickly the next day, though. Mitch snagged 5, ending their hopes of another strong performance with the bat.

Chris Rogers and Brad Haddin made half-centuries, but they were the only shining lights as we were bowled out for 204 the next morning. We were stung into action a bit: it was the first time we'd been behind after the first innings that series. We knew we needed to step up the bowling attack and it was Nathan Lyon who did the damage this time.

They were 6–172 at one point and we just ran through them to have them all out for 179 in a pretty amazing session of play. It was still a tricky target of 231 given the pitch had been doing a bit and we were batting last, but Chris Rogers was rarely troubled as he made an important century. We'd been tested more than at any point in the series. To head to Sydney 4–0 was testament to the determination of the boys to finish the job.

My knee had been getting progressively worse and there was some talk of me coming out of the side, but there was no way that was happening if I could help it. My knee was quite swollen, so I went to see David Young again and he drained it, then gave me another round of PRP injections.

We hadn't changed our line-up all series and we all wanted to lift that urn together. I managed to convince them I was right to go.

Alastair Cook won the toss for the first time that series and sent us in. It looked like a masterstroke at 5–97, but then Steve Smith and Brad Haddin put on a 128-run partnership. Even when Hadds was dismissed for 75, Smithy batted really well with the tail and made a ton in front of his home crowd. We made 326.

I think that lower-order fight-back really let the air out of the England boys' tyres; they probably thought they were going to bowl us out cheaply. They lost wickets early and often and were 5–23 before they struggled along to 155. Chris Rogers was the mainstay of our second innings with another classy century. We were bowled out just after lunch on day three at 448 runs in front.

All we needed was one last push.

Cook and Bell didn't stick around, but Michael Carberry was proving harder to remove. I was bowling when he shaped up for a backward defensive shot and his bat snapped right in half, which I'd never seen happen before. I'd like to think it was because of my express pace, but I think it's more likely that his bat had a pre-existing weak spot!

England were 3–87 at tea and I was thinking about getting up for a big day's play in the morning when things just started to come apart for them. Carberry went off Mitch's second ball after tea and the wickets just kept dropping. The boys made short work of them and England were 7–139 when I replaced Mitch Johnson.

Stokes dragged the first ball of that over back onto his stumps, then I bowled Broad early in the over after that. Hadds came up to me after I'd got Stokes and said he had a surprise for me, which I thought was odd. What could he possibly surprise me with out in the middle of the SCG?

I found out when the drinks came out onto the ground as Broad disappeared. I was cooked, so I took a big pull on my drink bottle and nearly threw up—Hadds had arranged to have my hydrolyte drink switched with cold beer. He thought this was hysterical and asked me how my drink was … I just looked at him, smiled and took another huge swig!

Boyd Rankin had been one of the three new faces in the England line-up for that Test and he was facing me two balls later. It was a decent ball on a good length, but he swung and nicked it to Michael Clarke at second slip to give us the win.

I found myself hugging my bowling partners Johnson, Siddle and Lyon, which was special because we'd all been through a bit. Then we ran over to the rest of the team to share in a moment that I don't know if I'll ever be able to describe adequately.

We'd experienced a few lows as a group while we were in England, but we'd bounced back in the most emphatic way possible. Winning back the Ashes meant everything to every one of those boys—we'd worked bloody hard to achieve that goal and there was no sweeter feeling.

Nathan Lyon, our song leader, got us in together on the pitch and we sang just about the most emotional 'Under the Southern Cross' I've ever been a part of.

It took a while for the presentations to get going, so we did a lap around the ground, which was brilliant. Everyone in the stadium stayed. The crowds had been absolutely outstanding all series. The boys often commented how loud and involved the fans were, and it was a great way to finish off. Even the Barmy Army gave us a decent send-off!

It was great to catch up briefly with the England lads on the ground and then have a beer with them later. It had been a hard-fought series that got a little tense at times, but we really respected them. I felt overall it was played in good spirits by both sides.

I finished with 8 wickets and got Player of the Match, which was the furthest thing from my mind (and actually a little embarrassing as I thought it should have gone to Chris Rogers). Mitch got the Player of the Series award, which he thoroughly deserved, but it would have been great if they could have split it between him and Brad Haddin. Hadds put in a huge series with the bat and the gloves, and it would have been a fitting reward.

It was an amazing feeling to stand up there with the rest of my brothers as Pup held the Ashes trophy over his head. We'd done it; we were all physically and mentally exhausted, but we'd done it.

CHAPTER 21

OVER THE LIMIT

Wellness.

Until a few years ago, if you had mentioned wellness to me, I would have assumed it was something they asked you about right before handing over some crystals, scented oils, a CD of ambient music and a complimentary psychic reading.

Well, if you excuse the attempt at humour, there's no making light of the whole 'wellness' gauge by me these days. Australian Cricket has taken huge strides with its approach to injury prevention with all the players around the country. Gone are the days when blokes would be the best judge of their own fitness, or a state physio would take care of pretty much everything from diagnosis to recovery.

These days, data is collected, crunched and then acted upon. Your pre- and post-game or training regimes include at least one spot of data entry into the AMS (Athlete

Management System), and you know that these regular inputs are examined and interpreted as to your wellbeing. It won't help you bowl an outswinger or fix a batting flaw, but the aim is to ensure that you are at your best physically and mentally, more often than not.

It's not an exact science, and when tied to selection availability (commonly known as the 'rotation policy'), can cause plenty of angst with players and fans alike. The first time I was 'rotated', in the West Indies in 2012, I was ropeable at first. But over the years, I have seen it from the other side too, and it has helped me and my captains with how they use me in matches.

I've been blessed to have played under some superb captains. At the Redbacks, my skippers included Boof, Nathan Adcock and Graham Manou, who was a mate before he was my captain.

In Queensland, I had Chris Simpson as my first captain and he was a thoughtful, innovative bloke who had a great feel for people. Since then, James Hopes has been the man with the Bulls and the Brisbane Heat, and he and I are definitely on the same wavelength. He bowled with 'hot spots' (effectively old or new stress fractures) in his back for much of the 2013–14 season and I know that he would never ask me to do something he would not ask himself to do first.

Ricky Ponting and Michael Clarke have very different captaincy styles, but both knew when to push and when to ease off and, importantly, when to protect bowlers from themselves. Michael was adept at taking input from so many different quarters—the coaches, the support staff, the players—and making the right call. It may not always have been popular, but inevitably it was the right call.

Here are a few numbers to help you get into this, from the numbers I put into our online player reporting system during the third Test match in South Africa.

RYAN HARRIS 'WELLNESS INDEX'

Test Match 1–5 March 2014*

	fatigue	sleep	soreness	stress	overall
1 March	4	2	4	4	4
2 March	4	3	4	4	4
3 March	2	4	1	2	2
4 March	2	5	1	2	3

*5 March: no information recorded—celebrations!

GLOSSARY

Fatigue
1. Always tired; 2. More tired than normal; 3. Normal; 4. Fresh; 5. Very fresh

Sleep
1. Insomnia — 5. Very restful

Soreness
1. Very sore — 5. No pain

Stress
1. Highly stressed — 5. Very relaxed

As you can see, I went from being fairly fresh to being in less-than-ideal shape. And as is the case with human nature, you tend to mark yourself lower the worse you are feeling.

Here are a few other numbers that are relevant. For the second and third Tests, several of us wore a GPS harness that tracked the distance we covered, whether bowling, in the field, or batting.

In the second Test I racked up 43 kilometres and the third Test I got 42 kilometres under my belt. That's a lot of short, sharp sprints and impacts, although nothing you don't prepare for through off-seasons, preseasons and regular conditioning.

Cumulatively, though, it was wearing me down.

By the time the third and final Test came around in Cape Town, my body was like one of those WWII bombers being nursed home from a raid, with bits and pieces falling off them from all of the flak damage as they limped back to base, finally flopping onto the tarmac with just fumes left in the tanks.

That Test was one where the Australian spirit was thoroughly challenged, and the efforts of our motivated and dedicated touring medical staff in overcoming the waves of walking wounded was nothing short of stupendous.

You couldn't go past the courage of Michael Clarke, whose battered and bashed limbs were aching from the working over he received at the hands of Morné Morkel and Dale Steyn during the first innings. He wore short balls all over—thumb, forearm, elbow, shoulder and head, with the blows to his shoulder enough to fracture it.

Getting hit by a cricket ball at speed is a unique and terrible sensation. As a bowler, I tend to inflict more than I get, but we all get hit. It doesn't really matter whether it is at training or in matches, the sensation remains the same.

It gets there fast and the impact is immediate. If it hits unprotected flesh or bone, you get a crushing sting, followed by a numbness that spirals outwards from the crash site.

That's only temporary though. The aching and deep throbbing usually follows hard on from that, as the outraged nerves in the area begin to spew out their frantic signals to your stunned brain.

If it has hit somewhere near the head, you are likely to be in a fog with your ears ringing.

If it has cut or grazed you, there can be an eerie delay as your addled senses work out whether the wetness is sweat or blood. If you can see it splattering on your clothes or the pitch, a degree of shock is normally not far away.

Even if it hits a piece of protective apparel, the outcome will be much the same.

Getting hit in the same place more than once heaps indignity upon the inevitable injury. The chink in your armour is being exploited by the opposition. As a bowler, you know you can get on top now.

Anyone who saw how relentlessly Mitch Johnson pursued the English and South African batsmen in 2013–14 can recognise that no matter how much courage a player can muster, or tells themselves they have to produce, self-preservation at a subliminal level will change how you play.

Picking up the pieces afterwards is the challenge that everyone faces. The best result is bruising. At least you know they fade.

Newcomers to cricket dressing-rooms are forgiven if they find their eyes drawn to the muddy patterns of healing bruises across the legs and midriffs of players as dressing or undressing takes place. 'Don't they hurt?' is the obvious question.

Yep, but not as much as when you get them.

Someone like Michael Clarke was as well equipped as anyone to deal with it. Targeting of captains by opposition teams is a trend, heck even a tactic these days. We'd successfully squeezed Alistair Cook during the Ashes and had some success keeping Graeme Smith away from big scores during this series.

Pup wore each of his blows, and when he gained the respite of the team rooms, with a century in his keeping, we all knew his defiance had given us a massive win.

The word 'tireless' should be somewhere on Alex Kountouris's business card. As physiotherapist to the team, his efforts sometimes seemed otherworldly. For someone whose well-meaning advice was often overlooked by certain head-strong cricketers who must surely know better, he was remarkably sane.

Having a team doctor on this trip was a godsend. Dr Peter Brukner was unflappable, no matter what was served up to him. A sports medicine specialist whose most recent engagement before us had been two years in the high-stakes world of the English Premier League with Liverpool, he tackled the lame and the ill with equal parts humour and quiet efficiency.

Part of me still shakes my head when I think of the number of tours that Australian teams have gone on in the past without a doctor on board.

I had been solid without being dominant in the first two Tests, and hadn't been terribly happy with my bowling. But as a group, we felt we were in top form coming into the last Test.

Towards the end of the third day, with South Africa only a few wickets away from being dismissed for 287, I had a few moments when despair hit.

Pup was asking me how I was and I didn't pretend. 'I don't think I can bowl another over', I told him.

I had been saying that to different people on and off during the series. My normal response when I am playing is that I say I am right to go whenever I am asked, whether I am or not, because by the time I get into the middle, I am so into the prospect of bowling that I end up being right. Adrenaline and anticipation tends to be good nerve blockers, and after that I am usually a fair judge of when I need a spell or whether I can keep going.

Damian Mednis, our big blond conditioner, had spent a fair bit of time with me at Queensland before joining the Aussie setup. An athlete himself originally, and with a background in Rugby Union before coming to cricket, he knew when to console and when to jolly you along.

We'd be at breakfast or waiting to get on the bus and the exchange would go along these lines.

'How are you H?'

'Yeah, not that good mate, I'm not sure if I can get out there this morning.'

'F*** off. Don't be soft.'

'Nah nah, it's no good mate.'

'Bull. Don't be late for warm-up.'

And then he'd wind up someone else or if his beloved Parramatta had managed to win an NRL match, he'd luxuriate in their brief success for a while as I shook it off, either with a laugh or a scowl depending on how sore I really was.

My confession to Pup gained me some respite off the field that afternoon, but deep down I knew I wasn't going to be able to quit. We took our 207-run lead and batted to stumps, finishing at 0–27, with the anticipation of a strong day four batting effort to set up a final day to bowl them out.

That night, the campaign to buy me two more days began in earnest. It featured a lot of poking and prodding, and it hurt. A lot. There were times I thought I was about to vomit as 'Lex' leaned in and tried to free up the tendons and muscles that were crying out for relief. The Doc was dry-needling my hip flexors, my hip and my abdominal muscles and there were moments when I basically could not lift my leg off the bench.

The physio room was doing double duty as a bunkhouse during that Test. Pup slept on the physio table at one stage, opting to rest where he was, until roused for more treatment.

My knee was not locked, but it was seizing up, and my running had begun to change. I was overcompensating and running more stiff-legged, trying to protect the knee. I was starting my run-up a bit earlier and trying to get the momentum going, and as I was doing that, the hip flexor began to flare up.

It was half-way through a game with the final surge to come. We knew there was plenty of time in the game to bowl them out but it was important that I could get out there with the others. When you are a bowler down, it is very hard to win games. The Newlands pitch was showing no signs of breaking up, so that wasn't going to make up for being one short.

As a bowler, there is no worse feeling than breaking down in the middle of a game when the game is there to be won. It had happened to me several times—with the Redbacks, with Australia at the MCG. The prize is there—you can see it—but the feeling of letting everyone else down overwhelms all else.

If I wanted to be there for the crowning glory of a South African series win after an Ashes triumph, for the biggest cold beer of the lot, then I ... we ... needed to find a way.

The morning of day four dawned. Like everyone, my wife, Cherie, knew that there was one gigantic push needed. I was trying not to be grumpy. I had got some sleep, not much, and was still very ginger. Getting on the bus I felt like I was battling to lift my leg up. I was pretty quiet.

The plan for the medical and coaching staff was simple. At whatever point the skipper was beginning to think about a declaration, give them an hour, or as much notice as possible, to get me and the other bowlers ready.

I had treatment the entire morning. Ice, dry-needling, stretching, rubbing, coupled with the now mandatory anti-inflammatories and painkillers. It was a day where our batting ebbed and flowed, but watching Dave Warner accelerate on the way to a slashing 145, his second big ton of the match after hitting 135 in the first dig, got the blood pumping in ways that the tireless hands of the medical and support staff could only dream about.

The tip on the declaration came. We got some tape where it was needed and everything moving in the right direction so

I was ready to warm up when we declared at 5–305 with a lead of 512 and a maximum of 142 overs to bowl. Adrenaline was in abundance but Pup and Boof took the extra time to make sure we were all focussed and knew our roles.

We had about thirty minutes to bowl, before tea, and then a final session to take us close to what we hoped would be a winning position on the final day.

Graeme Smith had announced this was going to be his last Test and both teams made sure his final innings was acknowledged with appropriate respect and appreciation. It's tough when you know that someone is in their last game, which obviously means a lot to them and their teammates, but is also standing in your way. We put that sentiment aside quickly, though.

I'd had a bit of success against the burly Proteas left-hander in this series but my breakthrough came a few overs in when I brought one back to trap Alviro Petersen in front to get the first of the 10 wickets we needed. Lost in all of this was the fact it was my 100th Test dismissal, and while the job remained to be done, I still had a moment to think of Mum, issue a silent sign to the heavens, before getting back to work.

Mitch followed the next over to bring down the curtain on Graeme Smith's career and then smashed through Dean Elgar's stumps to have them reeling at 3–15. But AB de Villiers, at the time probably the best or at least most consistent batsman in the world, wasn't going down without a fight. He and Hashim Amla fought hard either side of tea, but when young gun Jimmy Pattinson broke through to remove Amla and have South Africa 4–68, the home side looked unlikely to hold off our looming victory in the final session.

But AB kept going. He batted ... and batted ... and batted. For 326 minutes and 228 deliveries to be precise. Most of us were almost delirious with relief when I got a ball to move just enough to kiss the edge and be gloved by a grateful Brad Haddin. That dismissal opened the door for us, and Faf du Plessis and JP Duminy both fell (Steve Smith and Mitch doing the job for us). But the time was starting to evaporate and South Africa were perhaps one more dogged partnership away from holding us at bay.

There was drama too. We were convinced we had Vernon Philander caught off the glove from a brute of a short ball by Mitch. Umpire Aleem Dar gave it out, but it was overruled on review, which sparked the now infamous blue between Pup and Dale Steyn. I wasn't close enough to know how, what, or why ... but it left both men steaming. It was probably the angriest I had seen Pup since his exchange with Jimmy Anderson during the Ashes and again, flagging spirits were lifted. Mentally and physically, we were almost spent. All of those matches, all of that travel, all of that training, all of that pressure, all of that expectation, all of the relief that followed. No wonder we were having to grit our teeth. Pup was trying everything—one over stints, tying down one end and attacking from another.

The former Australian and Queensland quick Michael Kasprowicz—who knew something about having to perform under duress after almost bowling himself into the dusty

Indian wickets during Australia's 2004 tour—used to talk about the 'niggle worm'. It was the mysterious critter in a bowler's body that would move around, settling in a shoulder one moment, the back the next, the hip, the ankle. It was usually just enough to be uncomfortable and raise unwanted thoughts as to whether it was a sign of something serious or just the regulation aches and pains that come with regular physical labour.

Well this time, it had gone a bit past that—I was wrestling with a 'pain snake' that was striking any and everywhere the longer the game went on. You start off with a tender hamstring in the morning, notice an ache in your knee at lunch, and by the time you lie down to sleep in the evening, all you can feel is a sore back.

While I was treading a well-worn path endured by other Aussie quicks, Kasper's droll quip from that Indian series— that if he succumbed to the torturous conditions in the heat and humidity of the Subcontinent, at least he knew he would have died doing what he loved for his country—wasn't one I was especially keen to emulate.

I watched some highlights of the final days of the Test a few months later during my rehab at the National Cricket Centre. The first thing I noticed was that my run-up and action were nowhere near as ragged as I imagined they had been. I had felt like our dog Hank's favourite chew toy after a vigorous game of keep away, with nothing quite where it should be. Instead, I was getting to the crease relatively normally.

But when I saw myself walking back to the mark, the only thing I could think was that my wincing bow-legged gait reminded me of one of those weekend cyclists after they finish a lengthy ride on a Sunday morning.

Watching those final 5 overs, where we needed 2 of the final 3 wickets of Vernon Philander (who had got to 50 in pretty neat fashion), Steyn and Morné Morkel, I admit I was wondering where the breakthroughs were coming from again.

We just needed to keep in control. I could see the floodlights had been turned on, even though the light was still fine, but I guess that with there being every chance the match could be played through until the final moments, it was better to have them on if we went deep into the twilight.

Yes! Mitch strikes Philander on the pads—could this be the breakthrough? No sooner had the 'not out' been indicated than we had referred it for review. Again though, the third umpire disagreed with our assessment and the decision was not overturned.

Two balls later and the ball was back in my hand.

'C'mon Harry, time to pull the trigger.'

'One more effort Rhino. Big charge mate.'

'We've got this mob—we'll be drinking winner's piss soon. Go get 'em mate.'

I could barely register who was patting me on the back, or who was in my ear each time as I trudged back to the mark, wincing as I turned each time. But I kept going.

Just stay with it. Keep it simple and get the ball in the right area. Build the pressure, bowl with intent, keep it full and bring one back if you can.

Here we go. Steyn on strike, touch my chest, ignore the pain. Run in and let it rip.

And then the sound engulfed me. The ball had done what I had been striving to accomplish with it. It was full, pretty much a yorker, and it moved enough for the batsman to get an inside edge onto the stumps. Gone. We are back!

No pain now. Back to the mark. The slaps on my shoulders, back and bottom were vigorous. Morkel on strike and 5 balls in my over to go. Boof is up and down and seemingly everywhere on the boundary. Information is being pushed out and interpreted. It's going in, and being processed, but part of me is still gnawing away at how I can get this last wicket. The ball has been reversing and I think I can get them either leg before or bowled if I can put it where I want it. Here we go …

NO! I tried too hard and pushed it down leg, so the tall tailender was able to handle it without too much trouble. Morné is normally a fairly affable sort of bloke, with an easy smile, but a quick glance at him showed a strained and nervous face behind the grill.

And again. Ready at the mark, and in.

And this time, I can't hear the sound. It was fast, quicker than the previous ball, and it tailed back. It was full, and it reversed enough. He couldn't get the bat down quickly enough and the only thing it could hit was the stumps.

I think we charged around for a bit then. I honestly don't remember, other than the immense feeling of relief that washed over me after the initial wave of jubilation. A job well done.

I was nabbed by a journalist and asked what was going through my mind. I didn't think I could come up with anything profound, but I did offer that what we had just played was 'Proper Test-match cricket' and that it was bloody hard.

After being secretly disappointed that I hadn't bowled like I wanted to in the first two Tests, it was fitting that my best effort had come in the last Test, when my body was pretty much at its worst. The one thing that the 'wellness index' can't capture is the will within a person. You can have the worst night's sleep, be stressed, sore and out of sorts, but if your spirit and competitive instincts can drive you past that, then no amount of science can accurately determine if you should be playing. The good thing is that the team management and our sports scientists are on the same page— using the data we capture as a guide to ensure the players are best placed to perform more consistently for longer.

The light was beginning to be replaced by the artificial glow of the floodlights and I managed to check out the board. We had triumphed with just 27 balls left in the match.

What a finish to a game, a tour, a season, a summer … it will take something very special to top that in the years to come for anyone who was involved.

What a finish.

A COACH'S LIFE

I've talked about the people and coaches in my life who have made me the person and the cricketer I am today. And probably the reason I am drawn to coaching is that I would like to influence kids and other young players in the way that coaches have done for me.

But when it came to working out what sort of coach and mentor I would like to be, well … it was a bit of a challenge. Perhaps I should take bits and pieces from all of them? Some great Frankenstein's monster of a coach all stitched and patched together with new and old ideas? Combining old school and cutting edge, maybe I could blaze a new trail?

Or maybe I should look at the lessons learned along the way and see if I can impart the same simple qualities: make learning the game rewarding as well as enjoyable.

My first coach at primary school, Sean Watt, taught me

the basics of how to play the game. He taught, he encouraged, he corrected, he rewarded. Simple but effective stuff.

Peter Bajcic was probably the coach who taught me the most when I was young. He took fielding—which most kids perceived as something they did while waiting for a chance to bowl or bat—and made it special.

As I got older, and club cricket was my passion, I was influenced by Russell Thompson and Ian Morrison, two guys at Northern Districts who were passionate about the game and became two of my great mates. They also taught me as much about life as they did cricket. Respect on and off the field.

Tim Nielsen and Wayne Phillips invested a lot of time in trying to unlock the potential that they, and others, saw inside me. I didn't always see eye to eye with Flipper, but he always believed I had the ability to play at the highest level. Flipper, in particular, probably put more time than he should have in trying to get me to fly straight, and I guess that may have been to the detriment of others in the Redbacks system. He never gave up on me, though, and I remain very grateful to him for his persistence. It reinforces to me that a good coach should always do their best not to lose sight of the low-maintenance players in the group, because their well-being is just as important. I was lucky to have Tim again when he was with the Australian team and he hadn't changed. He pushed me hard and I copped my share of sprays from him over the years, but he was one of those determined and driven blokes with great feeling for the game.

At the SACA I had some excellent bowling coaches such as Andrew Sincock and Peter Muggleton. They helped me learn skills in areas of technique like ball release and grip, through to learning to find ways to relax when things weren't working. I probably frustrated the pants off them but they were always there to help.

As I became more attuned to what I had to do, and more confident, I started to learn more from the FBU—the Fast Bowlers United. I was first exposed to this when I arrived in Brisbane. Joe Dawes, the Queensland fast bowler, had created a mini-team within the team. Not a clique, but a group of other fast bowlers who basically worked together, socialised together, planned together and played together. We would do our own bowling planning sessions together so we each knew how we were going to bowl when we encountered the opposition. It didn't matter if you were a Test player or a rookie, you had input in those meetings. It is crucial to be a unit—Peter Siddle, Mitchell Johnson, James Pattinson and I made sure we were as tight as we could be during the 2014 Ashes series. If we hunted as a pack, it was better for the team. If the bowlers know each other like the backs of their hands, and have a strong bond, then the playing group benefits. Yes, you are competing for spots sometimes, and there will be times when you think you should be playing ahead of someone else. If you aren't where you think you should be, then look for the reason why and set about fixing it. Put the team first and when you do that, then you will find yourself part of a great team.

Joey and I gelled pretty much as soon I moved to Queensland. He was a late bloomer, and quickly became one of those blokes who the Bulls would rely on for 30-plus wickets a season, and usually more. He tormented the Redbacks, as he loved bowling to left-handers, and took me to another level. We tinkered with my action a bit, but his greatest influence was on my mindset. He taught me to think about what it was I was doing, every time I bowled. Not at the start of the over, or the middle of the over ... but every ball, whether in the most high-pressure match, or my first loosener at training.

Train with a purpose—it's the best advice I can impart now to young cricketers. It was something I had started to 'get' when I was in South Australia but it was really drilled into me with the Bulls. Bowling drills, medicine ball throws and trampoline drills to build core strength were all new to me. I wasn't a fan initially, but I took it on board, worked hard and ultimately benefitted.

These days, preventative recovery and training helps extend playing life. This is a message I am conscious of passing on to young bowlers now that I am dabbling with coaching. With young bowlers, it is almost inevitable that sometime between the ages of fourteen and twenty, they will have some form of injury. It stands to reason: the bones are still growing and hardening, supporting muscles are still reaching their peak, and the limits of training and playing workload thresholds are still largely unexplored. For young bowlers, it can be a big achievement to return from an injury, but some never make it back.

When it comes to training, you learn that there are areas you need to work on more than others. I learned from experience on that front: I tore a pectoral muscle early in my career with South Australia, which probably stemmed from doing too much upper body work and getting too big.

These days I know my legs, side, shoulder, Achilles and hip are areas that I need to work on, both to strengthen and to preventatively-rehabilitate them.

One thing I should stress about my approach to injuries, and management of the pain that goes along with them, is that I know the risks. I have made it my business to know what the treatment means and whether there are side effects. I trust the expertise of the people treating me, but I have learned to speak up if I think something is not right. I take the field at my own risk, and I look at whatever treatment options are available to me at my own risk.

Fast bowlers don't tend to have a uniform look. We tend to be functional rather than pin-ups. I reckon the last quicks who had the male model look were probably Brett Lee and Andy Bichel. Bic had real chiselled-out abs, big arms and chest, and he was powerful through his legs and trunk. He looked more like a footballer. Mitch Johnson is very athletic and powerful but he'd be the first to admit he can take or leave the calendar shots.

A few people have commented over the years that I can appear to look like I am carrying a few 'kegs' early in the season or tours. It's probably the case, as I have found that the more bowling I do, the thinner I get. I try to put weight on when I am not playing. I would rather start off a campaign around 96 kg, because I know I will end up around 91 kg or 92 kg by the end if I play all the games. You bowl two days out of four, 25 overs an innings at least ... your muscles get exhausted pretty regularly.

You learn your pain threshold along the way too. Where you can extend it, if you can extend it, or if you *want* to push it. You have to trust your medical and support staff and get to know them—which I tend to more often than not due to frequency of visits. I like to think I read them pretty well, and on the flipside I am upfront with them about what I think. By and large, I have been very fortunate. Physios such as Alex Kountouris and Kevin Sims with the Aussies, Adam Smith and Martin Love at Queensland, and John Porter at the SACA have been unstinting with sharing their knowledge and being prepared to work overtime. I reckon I have best patient–worst patient syndrome with them. Best in that I am normally there most days ... worst in that I will automatically take their recommended time of return from an injury and mentally knock a week or two off it. And then, of course, I get cranky when my estimate of four weeks turns out to be the six weeks they originally nominated.

On the occasions I have been injured in the latter stages of my career, I have been fortunate to have had a few chances to dabble in coaching, and also do some television and radio commentary. I can honestly say I enjoy elements of both, but they have also reinforced in my mind that I am not ready to call it quits just yet. Whether I end up going down one of those paths when I do stop playing is not something I have really thought through at the time of writing.

I've had a taste of coaching and assistant coaching teams—more at the work experience or unpaid intern level— and found it exciting and challenging. It is not as fulfilling as playing, but I am at that stage now where I realise that sentiment plays a part in how I feel about what lies beyond. Working with Australia A as an assistant coach during the winter of 2014 proved better than I thought. I was restricted to low-key rehabilitation so I really wanted to do the work with the players. One of the things I tried to adopt was to avoid the attitude that 'it's all about winning'. Instead, I looked at how the individuals were improving their skills.

I have also liked the one-on-one work I've done with some of the young bowlers in Queensland and at the National Cricket Centre. A few of them have spent more time injured than playing so far in their short careers, so I figure I am well placed to be able to offer some insights on how to walk along an often lonely path. They have to do some of it themselves, but they should know there is always someone who has trod the same track. As I push off my mark one more time, I can't help but wonder where cricket will take me next. I hope it is a path I am prepared for, but I am sure I am ready for it.

Ryan James Harris

Born: 11 October 1979, Sydney, Australia
Bowler right-arm fast – **Batsman** right-hand
Teams: Australia, Deccan Chargers, Kings XI Punjab, Queensland, South Australia, Surrey, Sussex, Yorkshire

Test debut: New Zealand v Australia at Wellington, New Zealand 19–23 March, 2010
ODI debut: Australia v South Africa at Hobart, Tasmania 18 January, 2009
T20 International debut: Australia v West Indies at Sydney, New South Wales 23 February, 2010
First-class debut: 2001/02
List A debut: 2000/01
Twenty20 debut: South Australia v Victoria at Adelaide, 1 January, 2007

Man of the Match Tests

Australia v West Indies 2011–12 at Bridgetown
Made 68* and 4* • Took 2–83 and 3–31
Australia v England 2013–14 at Sydney
Made 22 and 13 • Took 3–36 and 5–25

Man of the Series Tests

Shared award in the 2013 Ashes Series in England

Man of the Match ODIs

Australia v Pakistan 2009–10 at Adelaide
Made DNB • Took 5–43 off 10 overs (on debut)

Australia v Pakistan 2009–10 at Perth
Made 4 • Took 5–19 off 9.5 overs

Australia v England 2010 at The Oval, London
Made DNB • Took 5–32 off 8.4 overs

Career Statistics

(to June 2014)

All CRICKET

	M	Inns	NO	Runs	HS	Ave	50	CT	Overs	Runs	Wkt	Ave	SR	Best	5i	Econ
Tests	24	35	10	483	68*	19.32	2	11	830	2324	103	22.56	48.3	7–117	5	2.80
ODIs	21	13	7	48	21	8.00	0	6	171.5	832	44	18.90	23.4	5–19	3	4.84
T20Is	3	1	1	2	2*	–	0	0	11.4	95	4	23.75	17.5	2–27	0	8.14
First Class	76	115	19	1873	94	19.51	9	38	2529.2	7432	282	26.35	53.8	7–60	10	2.93
Sheffield Shield	46	75	9	1244	84	18.85	6	24	1550.3	4672	161	29.02	57.7	7–60	5	3.01
List A	85	51	19	411	39	12.84	0	33	689.1	3394	123	27.59	33.6	5–19	4	4.92
Aust One Day	63	38	12	363	39	13.96	0	27	508.2	2515	79	31.84	38.6	5–58	1	4.95
Aust Twenty20	64	37	15	239	31	10.86	0	23	235.3	1745	81	21.54	17.4	4–34	0	7.40

TEST MATCHES

Opponent	M	Inns	NO	Runs	HS	Ave	50	CT	Overs	Mdns	Runs	Wkt	Ave	SR	Best	5i
v NZ 2009–10	2	2	1	28	18*	28.00	0	1	70.3	13	207	9	23.00	47.0	4–77	0
v Eng 2010–11	3	5	1	14	10*	3.50	0	0	83.4	18	281	11	25.55	45.6	6–47	1
v SL 2011	2	3	1	33	23	16.50	0	1	66	25	160	11	14.55	36.0	5–62	1
v SA 2011–12	1	2	0	8	5	4.00	0	0	24.3	5	100	4	25.00	36.7	4–33	0
v Ind 2011–12	2	2	1	44	35*	44.00	0	0	78	21	179	6	29.83	78.0	3–41	0
v WI 2011–12	2	4	2	85	68*	42.50	1	2	62.4	12	184	6	30.67	62.6	3–31	0
v Eng 2013	4	7	2	99	33	19.80	0	2	162.1	37	470	24	19.58	40.5	7–117	2
v Eng 2013–14	5	6	1	117	55*	23.40	1	4	166.2	50	425	22	19.32	45.3	5–25	1
v SA 2013–14	3	4	1	55	26	18.33	0	1	116.1	39	318	10	31.80	69.7	4–32	0
Total	24	35	10	483	68*	19.32	2	11	830	221	2324	103	22.56	48.3	7–117	5

	M	Inns	NO	Runs	HS	Ave	50	CT	Overs	Mdns	Runs	Wkt	Ave	SR	Best	5i
Home	10	13	3	175	55*	17.50	1	4	328	90	883	39	22.69	50.4	6–47	2
Away	14	22	7	308	68*	20.53	1	7	502	131	1439	64	22.48	47.0	7–117	3

By Opponent

	M	Inns	NO	Runs	HS	Ave	50	CT	Overs	Mdns	Runs	Wkt	Ave	SR	Best	5i
England	12	18	4	230	55*	16.43	1	6	412.1	106	1176	57	20.63	43.3	7–117	4
India	2	2	1	44	35*	44.00	0	0	78	21	179	6	29.83	78.0	3–41	0
New Zealand	2	2	1	28	18*	28.00	0	1	70.3	13	207	9	23.00	47.0	4–77	0
South Africa	4	6	1	63	26	12.60	0	1	140.4	44	418	14	29.80	29.8	4–32	0
Sri Lanka	2	3	1	33	23	16.50	0	1	66	25	160	11	14.55	36.0	5–62	1
West Indies	2	4	2	85	68*	42.50	1	2	62.4	12	184	6	30.67	62.6	3–3	0

Batsmen dismissed most: AN Cook (England) 8, IR Bell (England) 7, KP Pietersen (England) 5, IJL Trott (England) 5, JE Root (England) 5.

Five wicket hauls in Test Cricket

	Overs	Mdns	Runs	Wkt
Australia v England 2010–11 at Perth	11	1	47	6
Australia v Sri Lanka 2011 at Galle	20	5	62	5
Australia v England 2013 at Lord's	26	6	72	5
Australia v England 2013 at Chester-le-Street	28	2	117	7
Australia v England 2013–14 at Sydney	9.4	4	25	5

ONE-DAY INTERNATIONALS

	M	Inn	NO	Runs	HS	Ave	50	CT	Overs	Mdns	Runs	Wkt	Ave	SR	Best	5i	Econ
ODIs	21	13	7	48	21	8.00	0	6	171.5	13	1031	44	18.91	23.4	5–19	3	4.84

Notes on ODI career: Took five wicket hauls in his first two ODIs, 3 Man of the Match awards, including his first two ODIs

SHEFFIELD SHIELD CRICKET – Season by Season

	M	Inn	NO	Runs	HS	Ave	50	CT	Overs	Mdns	Runs	Wkt	Ave	SR	Best	5i
South Australia																
2001–02	2	2	0	0	0	0.00	0	0	35.4	10	99	2	49.50	107.0	2–26	0
2002–03	5	9	1	81	27	10.13	0	5	131.3	25	384	10	38.40	78.9	3–64	0
2003–04	1	2	0	18	14	9.00	0	2	30	4	97	1	97.00	180.0	1–97	0
2004–05	4	8	0	161	47	20.13	0	3	113	23	395	9	43.89	75.3	4–92	0
2005–06	0															
2006–07	4	7	1	117	74	19.50	1	0	105.1	18	399	8	49.88	78.8	5–92	1
2007–08	10	18	3	363	60	24.20	2	1	372.2	94	1105	37	29.86	60.3	7–108	1
Queensland																
2008–09	8	14	2	206	51	17.17	1	4	279.5	64	874	33	26.48	50.8	4–59	0
2009–10	1	1	0	84	84	84.00	1	1	40	9	129	2	64.50	120.0	2–30	0
2010–11	2	2	0	8	8	4.00	0	2	78.3	20	208	15	13.87	31.4	5–72	1
2011–12	4	5	1	63	25*	15.75	0	4	154.1	53	359	20	17.95	46.2	7–60	1
2012–13	3	5	1	80	54*	20.00	1	1	143.2	38	423	19	22.26	45.2	6–58	1
2013–14	2	2	0	63	41	31.50	0	1	67	20	200	5	40.00	80.4	3–42	0
Total	46	75	9	1244	84	18.85	6	24	1550.3	378	4672	161	29.02	57.7	7–60	5

Batsmen dismissed most: GJ Bailey (Tasmania) 8, JW Wells (Tasmania) 6, TD Paine (Tasmania) 5, AC Voges (West Australia) 4.

	M	Inns	NO	Runs	HS	Ave	50	CT	Overs	Mdns	Runs	Wkt	Ave	SR	Best	5i
For South Australia	26	46	5	740	74	18.05	3	11	787.4	174	2479	67	37.00	70.54	7–108	2
For Queensland	20	29	4	504	84	20.16	3	13	762.5	204	2193	94	23.33	48.6	7–60	3

Five wicket hauls in Sheffield Shield

	Overs	Mdns	Runs	Wkt
for SA v WA 2006–07 at Adelaide	26.1	5	92	5
for SA v Tas 2007–08 at Adelaide	32	7	108	7
for Qld v Tas 2010–11 at Hobart	23	3	72	5
for Qld v Tas 2011–12 at Hobart	21.4	6	60	7
for Qld v WA 2012–13 at Perth	25.2	8	58	6

AUSTRALIAN DOMESTIC ONE DAY CRICKET – Season by Season

	M	Inns	NO	Runs	HS	Ave	50	SR	CT	Overs	Mdns	Runs	Wkt	Ave	SR	Best	5i	Econ
SA																		
2000–01	7	4	3	58	31*	58.00	0	98	3	36	1	216	5	43.20	43	2–29	0	6.00
2001–02	3	1	0	2	2	2.00	0	20	3	19	1	72	2	36.00	57	1–20	0	3.79
2002–03	3	2	1	2	2*	2.00	0	15	3	23	1	117	4	29.25	34	4–43	0	5.09
2003–04	4	3	2	10	9*	10.00	0	76	2	38	1	207	8	25.88	28	3–51	0	5.45
2004–05	8	7	1	80	26	13.33	0	59	3	72	7	329	10	32.90	43	2–31	0	4.57
2005–06	2	0				–			2	9	1	39	1	39.00	54	1–18	0	4.33
2006–07	8	6	3	41	13	13.67	0	105	1	73.5	1	382	11	34.73	40	3–49	0	5.17
2007–08	9	5	0	105	39	21.00	0	60	3	71.2	1	378	8	47.25	53	5–58	1	5.30
Qld																		
2008–09	9	5	1	34	22	8.50	0	89	3	75.2	5	311	9	34.56	50	2–28	0	4.13
2009–10	1	1	0	4	4	4.00	0	80	0	6	1	38	1	38.00	36	1–38	0	6.33
2010–11	2	1	1	13	13*	–	0	86	3	23	0	122	6	20.33	23	4–64	0	5.30
2011–12	1	1	0	8	8	8.00	0	133	0	13	1	57	1	57.00	78	1–57	0	4.38
2012–13	2	1	0	3	3	3.00	0	37	0	14.4	3	56	5	11.20	17	4–26	0	3.82
2013–14	4	1	0	3	3	3.00	0	37	1	34.1	2	191	8	23.88	25	3–61	0	5.59
Total	63	38	12	363	39	13.96	0	69	27	508.2	26	2515	79	31.84	38	5–58	1	4.95

TWENTY 20 CRICKET

	M	Inns	NO	Runs	HS	Ave	50	SR	CT	Overs	Mdns	Runs	Wkt	Ave	SR	Best	5i	Econ
IPL	37	21	9	117	17	9.75	0	104	20	138.4	3	1047	45	23.27	18	4–34	0	7.55
BBL	24	15	5	120	31	12.00	0	102	3	86.1	0	608	32	19.00	16	3–23	0	7.06
T20Is	3	1	1	2	2*	–	0	200	0	11.4	1	95	4	23.75	17	2–27	0	8.14
Total	64	37	15	239	31	10.86	0	103	23	236.3	4	1750	81	21.60	17	4–34	0	7.39